G08444

INFX3 (Line IVI)

Vulnerable Adult and Child Witnesses

The College of Law
of England and Wales

LIBRARY SERVICES

The College of Law, Braboeuf Manor, St. Catherines, Portsmouth Road, Guildford, GU3 1HA
Telephone: 01483 216788   E-mail: library.gld@lawcol.co.uk

**This book MUST be returned on or before the last date stamped below.
Failure to do so will result in a fine.**

Birmingham · Chester · Guildford · London · Manchester · York

Vulnerable Adult and Child Witnesses

Kevin Smith

and

Steve Tilney

OXFORD
UNIVERSITY PRESS

OXFORD

UNIVERSITY PRESS

Great Clarendon Street, Oxford OX2 6DP

Oxford University Press is a department of the University of Oxford.
It furthers the University's objective of excellence in research, scholarship,
and education by publishing worldwide in

Oxford New York

Auckland Cape Town Dar es Salaam Hong Kong Karachi
Kuala Lumpur Madrid Melbourne Mexico City Nairobi
New Delhi Shanghai Taipei Toronto

With offices in

Argentina Austria Brazil Chile Czech Republic France Greece
Guatemala Hungary Italy Japan Poland Portugal Singapore
South Korea Switzerland Thailand Turkey Ukraine Vietnam

Oxford is a registered trademark of Oxford University Press
in the UK and in certain other countries

Published in the United States
by Oxford University Press Inc., New York

British Library Cataloguing in Publication Data

Data available

Library of Congress Cataloging in Publication Data

Data available

Smith, Kevin.
  Vulnerable adult and child witnesses / Kevin Smith and Steve Tilney.
    p. cm.
  Identifying vulnerable and intimidated witnesses—Initial action—Offences commonly experienced by
vulnerable witnesses—Human trafficking—Multi-agency working—Special measures—Consent:
whose decision is it anyway?—Competence and compellability—Medical examinations—Witness
interview strategies—Planning and preparing for interviews—Conducting interviews—Storage and
retention of recordings—Ongoing protection orders—Witness intimidation—Pre-trial therapy—What's
on the horizon?"
  Includes bibliographical references and index.
  ISBN 978-0-19-921410-5 (pbk.: alk. paper) 1. Police questioning—Great Britain. 2. Interviewing in
law enforcement—Great Britain. 3. Child witnesses—Great Britain. 4. Witnesses—Great Britain—
Psychological aspects. 5. Witnesses—Legal status, laws, etc.—Great Britain. I. Tilney, Steve. II. Title.
  HV8195.A3.S615 2007
  363.25'40941—dc22
                                            2007028890

Typeset by Laserwords Private Ltd., Chennai, India
Printed in Great Britain
on acid-free paper by
Ashford Colour Press Limited, Gosport, Hampshire

ISBN 978–0–19–921410–5

10 9 8 7 6 5 4 3 2 1

Foreword

For too long the Criminal Justice System has excluded vulnerable people.

Children, people with mental health needs, people with learning disabilities, and others have been denied access to justice, as to treat them equally has been considered too difficult and too time consuming. It would be true to say that at some point each of the agencies within the criminal justice system have been guilty of this.

It is often said that we can judge a society by the way it treats its most vulnerable members. Moreover, unless vulnerable people have equal access to the criminal justice system, we don't have a justice system. Instead we have justice for some and not justice for all.

Things are changing. We now accept that vulnerable people have the same rights to justice as the rest of us. Kevin Smith and Steve Tilney are representative of a criminal justice system that is committed to promoting equality for all, whatever their needs and whatever their circumstances.

This important and timely book is a hugely practical and accessible guide to the law and best practice on all aspects of vulnerability in the criminal justice system. The authors have written from experience and from the heart. The book is valuable and important for all practitioners, and I am confident that the lessons learned from it will result in better outcomes for vulnerable people.

This book should be an essential guide for all those who believe in a fair and equal criminal justice system.

Kathryn Stone
Chief Executive, Voice UK
March 2007

Contents

Contents

Contents

APPENDICES

Abbreviations

ABE	Achieving Best Evidence
ACPO	Association of Chief Police Officers
BSL	British Sign Language
CJA	Criminal Justice Act 2003
CPS	Crown Prosecution Service
EPO	Emergency Protection Order
IRB	Intermediary Registration Borard
MCA	Mental Capacity Act 2005
OCJR	Office for Criminal Justice Reform
PACE	Police and Criminal Evidence Act 1984
POVA	Protection of Vulnerable Adults Scheme
PTZ	Pan Tilt Zoom (camera)
SOA	Sexual Offences Act 2003
SSE	Sign Supported English
YJCEA	Youth Justice and Criminal Evidence Act 1999

1

Identifying Vulnerable and Intimidated Witnesses

1.1 **Introduction**

Burton *et al* (2006) estimate that 54 per cent of all witnesses could be classified as vulnerable or intimidated and that 'on a very conservative estimate' some 24 per cent might be eligible for special measures. In contrast to this statistic, the police only explicitly identified 3–5 per cent of all witnesses as vulnerable or intimidated during the course of Burton *et al's* research, a figure that rose to 9 per cent when the researchers examined the case files. It would, therefore, seem that the police explicitly identify only a tenth of the witnesses who might be classified as vulnerable or intimidated and less than a fifth of those who could be eligible for special measures, leaving most vulnerable and intimidated witnesses to be identified as such by the Court Service and many of them without the benefits of special measures (such benefits were reported by Hamlyn *et al* (2004)). So what is going wrong? Perhaps an exploration of the history of the classification and treatment of vulnerable and intimidated witnesses, and the way in which the police are made aware of it, might help to shed some light on this issue.

1.2 **Background**

The fact that the criminal justice system regards certain groups of people as 'vulnerable' is not new. What has changed over the years is how the concept of vulnerability has been operationally defined and addressed. The Administrative Guidance to the Judge's Rules included an early attempt to standardize the way in which children (under 17) and anybody with a language difficulty were treated. Mental ability was not addressed at this time but it later became an issue for the Fisher Inquiry (1977) which, together with the Judge's Rules, influenced the Royal Commission on Criminal Procedure (1978 to 1981). The Royal Commission subsequently influenced the Police and Criminal Evidence Act 1984 and the Codes of Practice that accompany it, resulting in provision being made for appropriate adults to ensure the fair treatment of witnesses and suspected offenders defined as 'vulnerable' with reference to youth, language, or mental ability.

Increasing public concern about the high number of cases involving child witnesses which were not successfully prosecuted subsequently led to provision being made for those under 14 in cases of violence and those under 17 in cases involving sexual offences to give their evidence via live closed-circuit television link (s 32 of the Criminal Justice Act 1988). The intention behind such a provision was that it would go some way to reducing the stress experienced by the witness while giving evidence, resulting in an improvement in the quality of their testimony. In this sense, the Criminal Justice Act made the definition of vulnerability more complicated by linking the age of a child witness to particular types of offence. At the same time, the Government set up the Advisory Group on Video Evidence, chaired by Judge Thomas Pigot QC, to consider ways in which more cases involving child witnesses might be prosecuted. All this happened in parallel with several government inquiries into cases of child abuse, notably in Cleveland (published in 1987) where both the police and social services had been severely criticized for making use of inappropriate investigative techniques, including the use of leading questions in interviews.

The Home Office published what has become known as the Pigot Report in 1989. The report made a number of important recommendations that included provision being made for video-recorded evidence-in-chief and video-recorded cross-examination for child witnesses. It went on to suggest that these provisions be extended to other vulnerable witnesses in the fullness of time and that the definition of vulnerability be further developed to this end.

The first high-profile recommendation in the Pigot Report to be acted upon was the insertion of s 32A into the Criminal Justice Act 1988 by the Criminal Justice Act 1991, allowing those child witnesses who were already eligible to give their evidence via live closed-circuit television link to give their evidence-in-chief on a pre-recorded video. Guidance governing the conduct of these interviews was duly published in the form of the *Memorandum of Good Practice on Video Recorded Interviews with Child Witnesses for Criminal Proceedings* (Home Office, 1992). While the provisions set out in ss 32 and 32A of the Criminal Justice Act were applicable to child witnesses to any sexual and violent offence, the social context of the Cleveland Inquiry Report and the Orkney Inquiry Report (1992), still fresh in the minds of policy-makers, meant that in practice the emphasis was very much on joint working between police and social services in child protection cases.

The effect of ss 32 and 32A of the Criminal Justice Act and its operational emphasis on joint investigations in child protection cases was to create a two-tier system of the way in which child witnesses were treated. Children who were victims of or witnesses to child abuse perpetrated by a carer were usually interviewed on video. Such a video was subsequently played as evidence-in-chief and the child cross-examined by way of live television link. The same provision was in principle available to child witnesses in sexual or violent cases where the perpetrator was not a carer, but it was often confined to the more serious offences involving homicide or sexual assault perpetrated by a 'stranger' because those trained to interview child witnesses were predominantly child protection investigators and they were a limited resource. For other child witnesses, the provisions of Code C of the Codes of Practice to the Police and Criminal Evidence Act 1984 (PACE) still applied. Such provisions effectively meant that child witnesses deemed by the police as capable of making a written statement (with or without a declaration under s 9 of the Criminal Justice Act 1967) were interviewed in the presence of an appropriate adult.

By the mid 1990s, the treatment by the courts of another group of vulnerable witnesses, victims of sexual assault, had also become a cause for concern. Cross-examination by unrepresented defendants in person and the reluctance of the judges to afford these witnesses protection from the disclosure of their previous sexual history was a particular source of anxiety. These concerns, combined with a desire to further progress the recommendations made in the Pigot Report, were fuelled by research demonstrating the disproportionate extent to which vulnerable groups such as people with learning disabilities are victims of crime (see Westcott (1991) for a review of the literature). Such concerns were translated into manifesto commitments by the main political parties prior to the General Election 1997. The Labour Government set up an interdepartmental working group within a month of coming to power and the Home Office published the fruit of their endeavours in the form of the *Speaking Up for Justice* Report in June 1998. *Speaking Up for Justice* made 78 recommendations intended to help vulnerable and intimidated witnesses to give evidence. The first of these recommendations proposed a definition of vulnerability that was based on two categories: those vulnerable 'as a result of personal characteristics' such as a disorder or disability (referred to as 'category [a]' witnesses) and those 'whose vulnerabilities depend on circumstances' such as witnesses suffering emotional trauma or intimidation (referred to as 'category [b]' witnesses). While this categorization of vulnerability has undergone some refinement since 1998, it still underpins the definitions that investigators coming into contact with witnesses work with today.

The recommendations requiring legislation in *Speaking Up for Justice* were enacted in Pt II of the Youth Justice and Criminal Evidence Act 1999. This legislation defines 'vulnerable' and 'intimidated' witnesses (ss 16 and 17) and focuses on a number of provisions (eg restrictions on personal cross-examination by a defendant in sexual assault cases) and 'special measures' (eg the use of screens to prevent the witness seeing the defendant and vice versa) that are intended to help witnesses to give best evidence. Chapters I to V of Pt II of the Youth Justice and Criminal Evidence Act 1999 are reproduced in Appendix A for reference. In 2002, the Home Office published *Achieving Best Evidence in Criminal Proceedings: Guidance for Vulnerable and Intimidated Witnesses* (referred to as 'ABE' hereafter), a document that replaced and extended the Memorandum of Good Practice to take account of the new legislation and the developments in research and practice that had taken place during the course of the previous 10 years. A number of related Action for Justice programme publications, including *Vulnerable Witnesses: A Police Service Guide* (Home Office, 2002), were published at the same time. *Vulnerable Witnesses: A Police Service Guide* is of particular significance to this chapter because it sets out a number of prompts intended to assist the police in identifying vulnerable and intimidated witnesses.

1.3 **Witnesses**

Before considering how 'vulnerable' and 'intimidated' witnesses are defined in the Youth Justice and Criminal Evidence Act (YJCEA), it might be helpful to consider who witnesses are in a general sense. Witnesses are defined in s 63 of the YJCEA as: '... any person called, or proposed to be called, to give evidence in the proceedings'.

For practical policing purposes this means anybody, except a suspected offender, who is likely to give evidence in a trial. The implications of this are that people simply providing antecedent background information about the victim of a crime will not usually be regarded as witnesses unless they are in possession of some evidence about the offence (for example, a threat or a confession). On the other hand, the definition is clearly not restricted to direct eye or ear witnesses to the incident itself. The effect of this is that people in a position to provide circumstantial evidence that implicates a suspected offender will be witnesses (for example, people who witness the disposal of a weapon or other property associated with the offence).

The *Code of Practice for Victims of Crime* (Office for Criminal Justice Reform, 2005) adds further clarity to this definition when it draws a distinction between vulnerable victims and vulnerable witnesses. The Code does this by providing for an enhanced 'service' for vulnerable victims (paras 4.2 and 4.6) and enhanced 'support' for those victims who are likely to give evidence in court, ie witnesses (paras 1.6 and 5.8). From this point of view, the Code effectively defines victims as people who have suffered the effects of crime and witnesses as people who give evidence in court; not all victims are witnesses, not all witnesses are victims.

1.3.1 Vulnerable witnesses

The fact that legislation and Home Office guidance uses the term 'vulnerable' in relation to witnesses in at least two different ways is testimony to the complexity of defining the term. While the YJCEA, the Code of Practice for Victims, and the recent consultation draft Witness Charter (Office for Criminal Justice Reform, 2005) draw a distinction between 'vulnerable' and 'intimidated' witnesses, 'intimidated' witnesses are treated as a category of 'vulnerable' witness in *Speaking Up for Justice* (para 3.29), by *Vulnerable Witnesses: A Police Service Guide* (para 2.1), and the current edition of ABE (paras 1.3 and 3.1). When reading government publications it is, therefore, important to understand whether the term 'vulnerable' includes 'intimidated' witnesses or whether intimidated witnesses are regarded as a separate category.

While the inclusion of intimidated witnesses as part of a wider vulnerable category stems from the focus on circumstances that forms part of the definition in the original *Speaking Up for Justice* report, practitioners from the criminal justice agencies, notably the police and the Crown Prosecution Service (CPS), tend to use the term 'vulnerable' to refer only to those witnesses defined as such under s 16 of the YJCEA. 'Intimidated' witnesses (as defined in s 17 of the YJCEA) tend to be thought of as forming a separate category. This is probably the case because of the differences between vulnerable and intimidated witnesses in their eligibility for the 'special measures' (eg 'intimidated' witnesses are not eligible for aids to communication) and variations in the implementation timetable (eg video-recorded evidence-in-chief was not available to 'intimidated' witnesses at the time of writing).

'Vulnerable' witnesses are essentially those defined as such by virtue of their personal characteristics, as recommended in *Speaking Up for Justice*, plus those defined as vulnerable as a result of their youth. This definition is set out in s 16 of the YJCEA, as follows:

- All child witnesses (under 17); and
- Any witness whose quality of evidence is likely to be diminished because they:
  - Are suffering from a mental disorder (as defined by the Mental Health Act 1983); or
  - Have a significant impairment of intelligence and social functioning; or
  - Have a physical disability or are suffering from a physical disorder.

1.3.2 **Child witnesses**

Child witnesses are automatically 'vulnerable', although the extent to which they qualify for special measures as a result of this categorization varies according to the nature of the offence. Section 21 of the YJCEA effectively creates a sub-category of child witnesses 'in need of special protection' with reference to those who are witnesses in cases of 'sexual' or 'violent' offences. This focus on sexual or violent offences is similar to that in ss 32 and 32A of the Criminal Justice Act 1988, except that the upper age limit is set at 17 for both types of offence.

In the case of offences committed on or after 1 May 2004, 'sexual offence' means any offence contrary to:

- Part 1 of the Sexual Offences Act 2003; or
- The Protection of Children Act 1978 (as amended by s 45 of the Sexual Offences Act 2003).

In the case of offences committed before 1 May 2004, 'sexual offence' means any offence contrary to:

- The Sexual Offences Act 1956;
- The Indecency with Children Act 1960;
- The Sexual Offences Act 1967;
- Section 54 of the Criminal Law Act 1977; or
- The Protection of Children Act 1978.

'Violent offence' means:

- Any offence of kidnapping, false imprisonment, or an offence under ss 1 or 2 of the Child Abduction Act 1984;
- Any offence under s 1 of the Children and Young Persons Act 1933; or

- Any other offence involving:
  - Assault on;
  - Injury to; or
  - A threat of injury to a person.

The sub-category of child witnesses 'in need of special protection' is important because it has implications for the admissibility of their video-recorded interviews as evidence-in-chief in terms of the legislative provision and the implementation timetable.

1.3.3 **Witnesses vulnerable by virtue of a disorder or disability**

The court must take account of the views of the witness in determining whether a witness is vulnerable by virtue of disorder or disability (s 16(4)). In addition to this, when determining whether the quality of the witness's evidence is likely to be diminished in these circumstances, the court has to consider the likely completeness, coherence, and accuracy of that evidence (s 16(5)).

The legislation makes no distinction between:

- Those experiencing the effects of a life-long disorder or disability (eg Autistic Spectrum Disorder and Down's Syndrome) and those who experience such effects as a result of illness or injury in later life (eg the effects of a stroke or an injury sustained as a result of an assault or a road collision); or
- Disorders and disabilities that might fluctuate in their effects over a period of time (eg schizophrenia and other forms of psychosis) and according to the degree of stress arising from the social context.

In these circumstances, while the court will take account of the likely condition of the witness at the time of any trial, investigators should keep their options open at the time of the investigation by classifying the witness as vulnerable and, with the necessary consent, conducting the interview on video so that the possibility of video-recorded evidence-in-chief can at least be considered at a later stage.

Vulnerable Witnesses: A Police Service Guide (Home Office, 2002) sets out a number of prompts that are intended to help the police to identify vulnerable witnesses. These prompts fall into two groups: behavioural characteristics and physical characteristics. Behavioural characteristics include apparent difficulties in communicating or understanding, having a short attention span, being in an extreme emotional state (eg violent or withdrawn), and expressing strange ideas. Physical characteristics include unusual, uncontrollable, or hesitant movement of the body, head, or eyes. These prompts are not intended to be diagnostic of a disorder or disability. The Guide acknowledges that these characteristics might equally be accounted for by the effects of drugs or alcohol or that they could be due to external pressures arising from a stressful situation. In this sense, the prompts are intended to be used as a set of indicators that might merit further investigation when the circumstances of the witness and the case have been taken into account.

1.3.4 **Intimidated Witnesses**

'Intimidated' witnesses are those that are classified in *Speaking Up for Justice* as being vulnerable as a result of the circumstances. This classification has been developed by s 17 of the YJCEA where intimidated witnesses are defined as those whose quality of testimony is likely to be diminished by reason of fear or distress.

In determining whether a witness falls into this category, the court is obliged to take account of:

- The nature and alleged circumstances of the offence;
- The age of the witness;
- Where relevant:
  - The social and cultural background and ethnic origins of the witness;
  - The domestic and employment circumstances of the witness; and
  - Any religious beliefs or political opinions of the witness.
- Any behaviour towards the witness by:
  - The accused;
  - Members of the accused person's family or associates;
  - Any other person who is likely to be either an accused person or a witness in the proceedings.

Complainants in cases of sexual assault are defined as falling into this category per se by s 17(4) of the Act.

Vulnerable Witnesses: A Police Service Guide also lists a number of prompts aimed at helping the police to identify witnesses who are, potentially, intimidated. Given that intimidated witnesses are by virtue of the definition originally set out in *Speaking Up for Justice* those vulnerable by circumstance, these prompts focus on the:

- Nature of the offence (sexual offences, domestic violence, racially motivated crime, and repeat victimization);
- Relationship between the witness and the alleged offender (eg a carer);
- Living conditions of the witness (living in a place where there is a history of hostility towards the police or living in close proximity to the alleged offender or his or her associates);
- Background of the alleged offender (notably, where he or she has a history of violence or intimidation).

The Guide also suggests that elderly and frail witnesses should be regarded as intimidated when the court takes account of their age, as required by s 17 of the Act.

Since the publication of the Guide, the *Code of Practice for Victims of Crime* (Office for Criminal Justice Reform, 2005) has extended these prompts a little further by including the families of homicide victims in the intimidated category.

1.4 **Problems with Identification**

That relatively few vulnerable and intimidated witnesses are identified by the police and the CPS as such is, perhaps, not surprising for three reasons.

1.4.1 **Changing definitions**

The complex nature of vulnerability is such that the definition of vulnerability has changed over the years: from children under 17 and those with language difficulty to a more mature definition that also encompasses people with a disorder or disability and those in fear or distress of giving evidence. Such a definition has not simply developed in a cumulative fashion with the addition of new groups of witnesses. Its development has instead been rather messy at times with more restrictive definitions overlapping broader definitions, such as was the case when the limited provisions of the Criminal Justice Act 1988 stood in some contrast to the broader approach adopted in the PACE Codes of Practice, and such as is the case today where some definitions of vulnerability include intimidated witnesses while others treat intimidated witnesses as a separate category.

1.4.2 **Visibility**

The evaluation by Burton *et al* (2006) suggests that the police are more likely to identify vulnerable witnesses who might be considered highly visible (eg children and victims of sexual assault) than those who are not necessarily so visible (eg some witnesses with mental illness or learning disability). Such a lack of visibility is likely to be compounded by a societal stigma towards disability that motivates those able to do so to conceal any disorder or disability that they might have.

1.4.3 **Method of training**

Burton *et al* found that, with a few exceptions, most of the training aimed at improving the ability of the police to identify vulnerable and intimidated witnesses was done by means of distance learning, with no follow up classroom-based training. They found that this had little effect on police understanding and, thus, performance.

While it is accepted that the police will never be able to identify all vulnerable and intimidated witnesses, a position in which only a fraction of these witnesses are identified is untenable because:

- A failure to identify a witness as vulnerable or intimidated, where it is possible to do so, is unethical because it could increase the stress experienced by the witness in court as a result of denying them access to special measures;
- The criminal justice system is likely to be less effective because it is unlikely to consider the special measures and provisions that are intended to give the witness fair and equal access to justice;
- A failure to 'take all reasonable steps' to identify a vulnerable or intimidated victim as such might result in adverse comments being made by the court and disciplinary proceedings by virtue of the *Code of Practice for Victims of Crime* (such a provision might be extended in the future with the inception of a witness's charter).

The importance of adequate police training in the identification of vulnerable and intimidated witnesses cannot, therefore, be overstated.

1.5 **Chapter Summary**

The definition of 'vulnerability' is a complex one that has evolved over time and will undoubtedly continue to do so. The current definitions of 'vulnerable' and 'intimidated' witness are as follows:

- 'Vulnerable' witnesses are those under 17 and anybody of any age with a disorder or disability that is likely to diminish the quality of their evidence. These witnesses are vulnerable by virtue of their 'personal characteristics'.
- 'Intimidated' witnesses are those likely to be in fear or distress over testifying as a result of their circumstances or those of the offence (including the behaviour of the suspected offender).

Research suggests that police are poor at identifying vulnerable and intimidated witnesses. This situation must change for reasons associated with ethics, effectiveness, and policy.

SPACE FOR NOTES

SPACE FOR NOTES

Initial Action

2.1 **Introduction**

This chapter will deal with several different issues, which affect investigators and professionals alike. It is important that professionals appreciate the frameworks that govern the way in which they should deal with vulnerable adult and child victims, and that they are aware of the specific pieces of legislation and governmental guidance that relate to either vulnerable adults or children who are victims of crime.

2.2 **Legislative Frameworks for the Immediate Protection of Children: Police Protection**

Police protection is an emergency power bestowed upon the police by virtue of s 46 of the Children Act 1989. It enables police officers where appropriate to remove a child from a location to a place of safety for a period of up to 72 hours. The police do not have parental responsibility for a child when he or she is in police protection.

Once the child has been placed into police protection, no unauthorized person can lawfully remove the child from that location without the permission of the police, or social services if the child's care has been transferred from the police to social services.

Police protection is described as a 'one-off power' and should not be used again in relation to the same child when the 72 hours are up. If concerns about the safety of the child remain and the family have refused to work with social services during the 72 hours provided by police protection, social services will need to obtain an Emergency Protection Order (EPO) under s 44 of the Children Act 1989.

An EPO can last for up to eight days, but the local authority can approach the court and request that this order is extended. The order can be extended for up to seven days. When an EPO is issued by the court, an application can be made for the exclusion of a person or persons from an address as an alternative to removing the child. This can only be made if all the parties agree and the non-abusive partner undertakes to ensure that that person leaves and stays away.

Example—Police protection

It is Friday morning and the police are called to a local department store where a member of the public has found a three-year-old child wandering in the street outside. The police arrive at the store and speak to the child who says that mummy and daddy are asleep at home and there is no food for her to eat so she has gone to the shops to get some chocolate, she shows them a ten pence piece that she has in her pocket. Fearing that the child will

---

suffer significant harm if she is allowed to wander around alone, the child is placed into police protection and the social services are contacted. The duty social worker arrives and the police transfer care of the child to her or him. The child's identity and the family's address are established by making local enquiries and confirmed by a social services' records. The police visit the home address and find both parents suffering the effects of excessive alcohol intake. The parents are angry that the child is not at home and were unaware that she was missing; there are no other children at home. Both parents are arrested and interviewed, they are subsequently released on police bail while further enquiries are conducted.

What should happen next?
If there are still concerns over the safety of the child if she is returned home, social services will try to accommodate the child with a suitable extended family member. If there is no suitable extended family member or the child's parents will not agree to having the child accommodated elsewhere on a voluntarily basis and there is a likelihood that the child will suffer significant harm if she is returned to her parents, social services will contact their legal department to go to court and get an EPO.

The police have several tasks that must be completed by them in respect of the police protection. They should:

- Ensure that the child is taken to a place of safety and that the child is not removed from that place;
- Inform the local authority where the child is found;
- Inform the local authority where the child lives;
- Inform the child if he or she is able to understand; and
- Ascertain the child's wishes, if possible.

A designated officer should be allocated to inquire into the circumstances in which the child came to be in police protection. Such a designated officer is a police officer of at least the rank of inspector. The police should talk to the child's:

- Parent(s) or guardian and any other person who may have parental responsibility for the child; and
- Anybody else who the child was staying with before taken into police protection;

about what has happened and inform them of any further steps that may be taken. When this has been done, the designated officer should release the child from police protection unless it is considered that there are still reasonable grounds for believing that the child will suffer, or will be likely to suffer from significant harm.

While a child is being kept in police protection, the designated officer may make an application on behalf of the Local Authority for an EPO under s 44 of the Children Act 1989.

The designated officer is responsible for promoting and safeguarding the child's welfare, while the child is in police protection. While in police protection, the designated officer should also allow the child to see his or her parent(s), guardian, any other person who has parental responsibility for the child, or anybody who has an order issued by the court under s 34 of the Children Act 1989, provided that such contact is in the child's best interests and is reasonable.

2.3 Non-Legislative Frameworks for the Protection of Vulnerable Adults

At present, there is no one piece of legislation which directly protects vulnerable adults. In the absence of such legislation, the relevant appropriate powers and duties for intervention are found in a range of legislation and guidance.

The police and local authorities have a statutory responsibility to ensure that concerns about the care and welfare of vulnerable adults are thoroughly investigated.

At a local level, all agencies who are involved in the protection of vulnerable adults are beginning to start to work together to ensure that the correct policies and procedures are adopted and put into place to help to effect these changes. To this end, there are several government initiatives that will go some way to address the issues around the protection of vulnerable adults.

2.3.1 Protection of Vulnerable Adults (POVA)

In England and Wales, the Protection of Vulnerable Adults Scheme (POVA) for care homes and domiciliary care agencies has brought in a list of workers who have abused or harmed a vulnerable adult, or put that person at risk of abuse or harm.

The purpose of this list is to make sure that people who are known to abuse will not be able to gain employment in the private or public sector working with vulnerable adults.

POVA will enhance the pre-employment process; this will include Criminal Records Bureau checks, which already take place and stop known abusers from working or caring for vulnerable adults. It is intended that POVA will complement other government initiatives, for example: *No Secrets* (Department of Health, 2000) and *In Safe Hands* (National Assembly for Wales, 2000).

POINT TO NOTE—THE IMPORTANCE OF THE POVA SCHEME

Sadly, in recent years, there have been too many instances where vulnerable adults have been harmed in situations where they should have protected by either professionals or family members, in care setting or their own homes.

For their part, as the POVA scheme is implemented, councils with social services responsibilities and their local NHS and police force partners, should not under-estimate the important work they have done, and need to do, with regard to *No Secrets* and *In Safe Hands*.

In particular, they should ensure that the general public is made aware of adult abuse and what to do if they experience it or see it.

By working together, we can make sure that vulnerable adults get the respect and care that they deserve. I am sure that providers of care and other stakeholders will work hard to ensure that the POVA scheme is a success.

Stephen Ladyman
Minister for Community Care

2.3.2 *No Secrets* and *In Safe Hands*

No Secrets is the government guidance on developing and implementing multi-agency policies and procedures to protect vulnerable adults from abuse in England. *In Safe Hands* is the Welsh equivalent of *No Secrets*. It contains policies and procedures that have been tailored to fit the requirements of local government in Wales.

The guidance contained in *No Secrets* and *In Safe Hands* applies to all vulnerable people who are 18 years of age or over, and requires local authority departments described under s 7 of the Local Authority Social Services Act 1970 to develop and co-ordinate multi-agency procedures and policies that will protect vulnerable adults.

There have been policies and procedures in place for a number of years which relate to the protection of persons who are vulnerable by virtue of their age (children and young persons). New and robust policies that are focused on the protection of adults will complement the existing strategies already in existence.

When police investigators or members of a local authority are making decisions about what action they should take, the rights of vulnerable adults to make choices, decisions, and calculated risks, and of their capacity to make such informed decisions about arrangements for investigation or management of an abusive situation, must be taken into account.

Explanation of capacity

Any person is presumed to have the capacity to make decisions for themselves unless they:

- Are unable to understand and remember relevant information in relation to decisions, and as to the impact and consequences of either making or not making that decision; or
- Are unable to believe the information; or
- Are unable to consider all the available information as a whole when arriving at a balanced decision.

It should also be noted that any assessment as to a person's capacity has to be made in relation to a [specific] proposal.

The Law Commission recommends that anything done for, and any decision made on behalf of a person without capacity, should be done or made in the best interests of that person.

In order to assist in deciding what is in a person's best interests, the Law Commission suggested a 'checklist' which is intended to be flexible.

- The ascertainable past and present wishes and feelings of the person concerned and the factors that person would consider if able to do so.
- The need to permit and encourage the person to participate, or to improve his or her ability to participate, as fully as possible in anything done for and any decision affecting him or her.
- The views of other people whom it is appropriate and practicable to consult about the person's wishes and feelings and what would be in his or her best interests.
- Whether the purpose for which any action or decision is required can be as effectively achieved in a manner less restrictive of the person's freedom of action.

2.3.3 Other agency involvement

Health Service

All staff working within the remit of the National Health Service and private health care organizations have an important role in recognizing and referring any suspected abuse or maltreatment of vulnerable persons.

Education

Some young adults will remain in mainstream education until age 19; vulnerable adults can attend Further Education establishments. Teachers, lecturers, and assistants will also have an important role to play in the recognition and referral of suspected abuse or mistreatment.

2.4 Extent and Potential Consequences of Pre-Interview Contact

It is a fact of life that investigators will always need to have some level of involvement with witnesses before and after an evidential statement has been taken, regardless of the format that the statement takes. Pre-interview meetings with witnesses will need to be carefully managed if allegations of coaching by the defence are to be avoided.

Where investigators or other professionals have such contact, a detailed record will need to be kept of such matters as when, where, who was present, what was said, and if any investigative decisions are reached as a result of meetings.

The obvious reason for a pre-interview meeting will be for the interview team to introduce themselves to the witness and to enable any assessment of competence or cognitive ability to be undertaken, or to assess any medical needs of the witness. This will be a particular requirement if an intermediary is to be involved in the interview process, as an assessment will form an integral part of their role.

2.5 Chapter Summary

This chapter has dealt with initial action following the identification of a vulnerable witness. In the case of children, much of this is governed by the statutory frameworks set out in the Children Act 1989. In the case of vulnerable adults, much of this is governed by the non-statutory frameworks of POVA and in the guidance set out in *No Secrets* and *In Safe Hands*. Both the statutory and non-statutory frameworks are multi-agency in their nature.

It is important for police investigators and other professionals alike to understand the different roles and constraints under which agencies work in order to prevent any misunderstanding that could ultimately affect the way in which investigators and other professionals deal with a given set of circumstances.

SPACE FOR NOTES

SPACE FOR NOTES

SPACE FOR NOTES

Offences Commonly Experienced by Vulnerable Witnesses

3.1 **Introduction**

Research suggests that vulnerable groups such as people with learning disabilities are more likely than most of the population to be victims of crime (see Westcott, 1991, for a review of the literature). While it is true to say that vulnerable witnesses experience a variety of offences along with the rest of the population, the kind of offences they are most likely to experience and that concern us most are those relating to sexual matters or personal violence. For this reason, this chapter briefly outlines the sexual and violent offences, including cruelty and neglect, most commonly experienced by vulnerable witnesses.

Rather than quoting extensively from statute, this chapter paraphrases the legislation in commentary to render it more accessible to the reader.

3.2 **Sexual Offences**

The sexual offences referred to in this part of the chapter relate to acts committed on or after 1 May 2004. With the exception of the offences relating to indecent photographs of children, these offences are all contrary to the legislation set out in Pt 1 of the Sexual Offences Act 2003 (SOA).

When investigating acts alleged to have been committed before this date, investigators will need to refer to the Sexual Offences Act 1956 and to disregard the amendment to the age parameters for offences relating to indecent photographs of children that was inserted by the 2003 Act.

The penalties for these offences are not shown in this chapter because, following the implementation of the Serious Organised Crime and Police Act 2005, they make little difference to investigative decision-making. All these offences can be tried in the Crown Court: some can only be tried in the Crown Court, while others can be tried either in the Magistrates' or the Crown Court depending on the circumstances.

3.3 **Sexual Offences: Interpretations and Consent**

The sexual offences referred to under the SOA 2003 share a number of common interpretations. These interpretations are defined in ss 78 and 79:

- Penetration, touching or any other activity is sexual if a reasonable person would consider that:
  (a) ... it is because its nature is sexual; or
  (b) It might be sexual because of the circumstances or intent.
- Penetration is a continuing act from entry to withdrawal.
- References to a part of the body include references to a part surgically constructed, in particular, through gender reassignment surgery.

- Image means a moving, still or three-dimensional image produced by any means. References to an image of a person include references to an image of an imaginary person.
- References to observation (however expressed) are to observation, whether direct or by looking at an image.
- Touching includes touching:
  (a) With any part of the body;
  (b) With anything else;
  (c) Through anything;
  and, in particular, includes touching amounting to penetration.
- Vagina includes vulva.

According to s 74, a person 'consents' if he or she agrees by choice and has the freedom and the capacity to make that choice. Section 75 states that a complainant to a sexual offence will not be considered to have consented if:

- At the time of the alleged offence or immediately before it began, any person:
  - Used violence against the complainant;
  - Caused the complainant to fear that immediate violence would be used against him or her;
  - Caused the complainant to fear that violence was being used against another person;
  - Caused the complainant to fear that immediate violence would be used, against another person;
- The complainant was, and the alleged offender was not, unlawfully detained at the time of the offence;
- The complainant was asleep or otherwise unconscious at the time of the alleged offence;
- The complainant could not communicate consent as a result of physical disability;
- Any person administers or causes the complainant to take a substance without their consent that is capable of causing or enabling them to be stupefied or overpowered at the time of the offence.

In addition to this, in s 76, consent is negated in relation to the offences set out in s 1 to 4 of the Act where the alleged offender intended to deceive the complainant as to the nature or purpose of the act, and he or she intended to induce the complainant to consent to the act by impersonating a person known personally to the complainant.

3.4 **Sexual Offences: General**

The offences set out in s 1 to 4 and 61 of the SOA 2003 have a broad application in that any person, including vulnerable people, may fall victim to them.

3.4.1 **Section 1 Rape**

A person commits this offence if he intentionally penetrates the vagina, anus, or mouth of another person with his penis in circumstances where the other person does not consent and the offender does not reasonably believe that the other person consents.

While this offence is usually committed by a male, by virtue of the fact that it involves penetration by a penis, it is possible for a female to be convicted of rape if it can be shown that she was involved in the offence to the point of having a common cause with a male offender.

3.4.2 **Section 2 Assault by penetration**

A person commits this offence if he or she intentionally penetrates the vagina or anus of another person with a part of his body or with anything else, provided that the penetration is sexual, and that the other person does not consent and the offender does not reasonably believe that the other person consents.

3.4.3 **Section 3 Sexual assault**

A person commits this offence if he or she intentionally touches another person, provided that the touching is sexual, and that the other person does not consent and the offender does not reasonably believe that the other person consents.

3.4.4 **Section 4 Causing a person to engage in sexual activity without consent**

A person commits this offence if he or she intentionally causes another person to engage in a sexual activity, the other person does not consent and the offender does not reasonably believe that the other person consents.

3.4.5 **Section 61 Administering a substance with intent**

A person commits an offence if he or she intentionally administers a substance to, or causes a substance to be taken by, another person without their consent and with the intention of stupefying or overpowering them so as to enable any person to engage in a sexual activity involving them.

3.5 **Sexual Offences: Committed Against Children Under 13**

The offences set out in ss 5 to 8 of the SOA 2003 largely replicate those set out in ss 1 to 4 of the Act. The principle difference in respect of offences committed against children under 13 is that the tender age of the victim is such that the absence of consent does not have to be explicitly proved to merit a charge.

3.5.1 **Section 5 Rape of a child under 13**

A person commits this offence if he intentionally penetrates the vagina, anus or mouth of a child under 13 with his penis.

As with s 1 rape, while this offence is usually committed by a male, by virtue of the fact that it involves penetration by a penis, it is possible for a female to be convicted of raping a child under 13 if it can be shown that she was involved in the offence to the point of having a common cause with a male offender.

3.5.2 **Section 6 Assault of a child under 13 by penetration**

A person commits this offence if he or she intentionally penetrates the vagina or anus of a child under 13 with a part of his body or with anything else and the penetration is sexual.

3.5.3 **Section 7 Sexual assault of a child under 13**

A person commits this offence if he or she intentionally touches a child under 13 and the touching is sexual.

3.5.4 **Section 8 Causing or inciting a child under 13 to engage in sexual activity**

A person commits this offence if he or she intentionally causes a child under 13 to engage in a sexual activity.

3.6 **Child Sex Offences**

The child sex offences set out in ss 9 to 13 of the SOA 2003 refer to sexual activity with or in the presence of children who are either under 13, or under 16 unless the alleged offender reasonably believes them to be 16 or over.

3.6.1 **Section 9 Sexual activity with a child**

A person who is 18 or over commits an offence if he or she intentionally touches a child and the touching is sexual.

3.6.2 **Section 10 Causing or inciting a child to engage in sexual activity**

A person who is 18 or over commits an offence if he or she intentionally causes or incites a child to engage in a sexual activity.

3.6.3 Section 11 Engaging in sexual activity in the presence of a child

A person who is 18 or over commits an offence if he or she intentionally engages in a sexual activity and, for the purpose of obtaining sexual gratification, does so:

(a) When a child is either present or is in a place from which the sexual activity can be observed;

(b) In the knowledge, belief or intention that the child is aware of it.

3.6.4 Section 12 Causing a child to watch a sexual act

A person who is 18 or over commits an offence if, for the purpose of obtaining sexual gratification, he or she intentionally causes a child to watch a third person engaging in a sexual activity or to look at an image of a person engaging in a sexual activity.

3.6.5 Section 13 Child sex offences committed by children or young persons

A person under 18 commits an offence if he or she does anything which would be an offence under any of ss 9 to 12 if he or she were aged 18.

The purpose of this section is to reduce the penalty for child sex offenders, although all these offences can still be tried either in the Magistrates'/Youth Court or the Crown Court.

3.6.6 Section 14 Arranging or facilitating the commission of a child sex offence

A person commits an offence if he or she intentionally arranges or facilitates something that he intends to do, intends another person to do, or believes that another person will do, in any part of the world that involves the commission of an offence under any of ss 9 to 13.

A person does not commit an offence under this section if he or she arranges or facilitates something that he or she believes another person will do to protect the child.

3.6.7 Section 15 Meeting a child following sexual grooming, etc.

A person who is 18 or over commits an offence if, having met or communicated on at least two earlier occasions with a child who is under 16 that they do not reasonably believe to be 16 or over, he or she:

(a) Intentionally meets or travels with the intention of meeting that child in any part of the world; and

(b) At the time, intends to do anything to or in respect of the child during or after the meeting that involves the commission of an offence in Pt 1 of the Sexual Offences Act 2003 or any other offence specified in Sch 3 to the Act.

Behaviour outside England and Wales that would amount to an offence if it occurred in England and Wales also falls within the scope of this section.

3.7 **Abuse of a Position of Trust**

The offences of abusing a position of trust set out in ss 16 to 19 of the SOA 2003 relate to people who look after children under 18 in a variety of institutional settings.

Where the child is 13 or older an offence is not committed if the alleged offender reasonably believes them to be 18 or over.

The phrase 'position of trust' is fairly wide ranging and is described in detail in ss 21 and 22 of the SOA 2003. Briefly, it includes settings in which the offender looks after the child in:

- A young offenders' institution or a prison;
- Accommodation provided by a local authority;
- Accommodation provided by a voluntary organization;
- A hospital;
- An independent clinic;
- A care home, residential care home, or private hospital;
- A community home, voluntary home, or children's home;
- A residential family centre;
- An educational institution.

Exemptions from the offences set out in ss 16 to 19 of the SOA exist where the parties concerned are lawfully married or had a lawful sexual relationship pre-dating the position of trust (ss 23 and 24).

3.7.1 **Section 16 Abuse of a position of trust: sexual activity with a child**

A person who is 18 or over commits an offence if he or she sexually touches a child with the intention of doing so while he or she knows, or could reasonably be expected to know, that he or she is in a position of trust in relation to the child.

3.7.2 **Section 17 Abuse of a position of trust: causing or inciting a child to engage in sexual activity**

A person who is 18 or over commits an offence if he or she intentionally causes or incites a child to engage in a sexual activity while he or she knows, or could reasonably be expected to know, that he or she is in a position of trust in relation to the child.

3.7.3 Section 18 Abuse of a position of trust: sexual activity in the presence of a child

A person who is 18 or over commits an offence if he or she intentionally engages in a sexual activity and, for the purpose of obtaining sexual gratification, does so:

(a) When a child is either present or in a place from which the sexual activity can be observed;
(b) In the knowledge of, or with the belief, or intention that the child is aware of it;
(c) While he or she knows, or could reasonably be expected to know, that he or she is in a position of trust in relation to the child.

3.7.4 Section 19 Abuse of a position of trust: causing a child to watch a sexual act

A person who is 18 or over commits an offence if he or she intentionally causes a child to watch a third person engaging in a sexual activity or to look at an image of a person engaging in a sexual activity for the purpose of obtaining sexual gratification while he or she knows, or could reasonably be expected to know, that he or she is in a position of trust in relation to the child.

3.8 Familial Child Sex Offences

The familial child sex offences set out in ss 25 and 26 of the SOA 2003 relate to people who are related to children under 18 in a number of specified ways.

Where the child is 13 or older an offence is not committed if the alleged offender reasonably believes them to be 18 or over.

The relationships covered by the familial child sex offences set out in ss 25 and 26 are described in detail in s 27 of the SOA 2003. Briefly they are:

(1) Where the relationship between offender and the child is such that one of them is the other's:
  • Parent (including past and present foster-parents);
  • Grandparent;
  • Brother (including half-brother);
  • Sister (including half-sister);
  • Aunt (the sister or half-sister of the other's parent); or
  • Uncle (the brother or half-brother of the other's parent).
  These relationships include those that have arisen through adoption other than where a lawful sexual relationship pre-dates the adoption (s 29).

(2) Where the offender and the child live or have lived in the same household or where the offender has been regularly involved in caring for, training, supervising, or being in sole charge of the child, it also includes situations in which offender is the child's:
- Cousin;
- Step-parent (past or present);
- Step-brother (past or present);
- Step-sister (past or present).

(3) Where the offender and the child live in the same household and he or she is regularly involved in caring for, training, supervising or being in sole charge of the child.

An exemption from the offences set out in ss 25 and 26 exists where the parties concerned are lawfully married (s 28).

3.8.1 Section 25 Sexual activity with a child family member

A person commits an offence if he or she intentionally touches a child family member and the touching is sexual.

3.8.2 Section 26 Inciting a child family member to engage in sexual activity

A person commits an offence if he or she intentionally incites a child family member to touch, or allow him or herself to be touched by the offender and the touching is sexual.

3.9 Abuse of Children through Prostitution and Pornography

The offences set out in ss 47 to 50 of the SOA 2003 relate to people who abuse children under 18 through prostitution or pornography.

Where the child is 13 or older an offence is not committed if the alleged offender reasonably believes them to be 18 or over.

A 'prostitute' is a person who, on at least one occasion and whether or not compelled to do so, offers or provides sexual services to another in return for payment or a promise of payment. Payment means any financial advantage, including the discharge of an obligation to pay or the provision of goods or services (including sexual services) gratuitously or at a discount.

A person is involved in 'pornography' if an indecent image of that person is recorded.

3.9.1 Section 47 Paying for sexual services of a child

A person commits an offence if he or she intentionally obtains for him or herself the sexual services of a child and, before obtaining those services, has made or promised payment for those services to the child or a third person, or knows that another person has made or promised such a payment.

3.9.2 Section 48 Causing or inciting child prostitution or pornography

A person commits an offence if he or she intentionally causes or incites a child to become a prostitute, or to be involved in pornography, in any part of the world.

3.9.3 Section 49 Controlling a child prostitute or a child involved in pornography

A person commits an offence if he or she intentionally controls any of the activities of a child that relate to prostitution or involvement in pornography in any part of the world.

3.9.4 Section 50 Arranging or facilitating child prostitution or pornography

A person commits an offence if he or she intentionally arranges or facilitates the prostitution or involvement in pornography in any part of the world of a child.

3.10 Indecent Photographs or Pseudo-Photographs of Children

Section 45 of the SOA 2003 raised the age limit from 16 to 18 for the offences relating to indecent photographs or pseudo-photographs of children under s 1 of the Protection of Children Act 1978 and s 160 of the Criminal Justice Act 1988.

Section 45 also creates an exemption from the offences set out in s 1 of the Protection of Children Act and s 160 of the Criminal Justice Act which exists where the child is 16 or over and is lawfully married or lives with the other person as partners in an enduring family relationship. This exemption only applies where the photograph is either of the child alone or only of the child and the person they are married to or living with as partners.

Whether a photograph or pseudo-photograph is 'indecent' or not is a matter for the court.

'Indecent photographs' include photographs, films, indecent photographs in films, negatives, and electronic data that is capable of being converted into a photograph or any form of video-recording.

Pseudo-photographs are images that appear to be a photograph that was created by computer graphics or otherwise. Pseudo-photographs include electronic data that is capable of being converted into a photograph.

3.10.1 Section 1 of the Protection of Children Act 1978 (as amended): taking, distributing or showing indecent photographs or pseudo-photographs of children

A person commits an offence if he or she:

- Takes or permits to be taken or makes any indecent photograph or pseudo-photograph of a child;
- Distributes or shows any indecent photograph or pseudo-photograph of a child;
- Possesses any indecent photograph or pseudo-photograph of a child with a view to distributing or showing it; or
- Publishes or causes to be published any advertisement likely to be understood as conveying the impression that the advertiser distributes or shows indecent photographs of a child or intends to do so.

3.10.2 Section 160 of the Criminal Justice Act 1988 (as amended): possessing indecent photographs or pseudo-photographs of children

A person commits an offence if he or she possesses any indecent photograph or pseudo-photograph of a child.

3.11 Sexual Offences Against People with a Mental Disorder Impeding Choice

The sexual offences against people with a mental disorder impeding choice that are set out in ss 30 to 33 of the SOA 2003 relate to people who are unable to refuse an offender's behaviour for a reason related to mental disorder. A person is considered unable to refuse if:

- He or she lacks the capacity to agree to the offender's behaviour; or
- He or she is unable to communicate a choice to the offender.

According to s 79 of the SOA 2003, the term 'mental disorder' has the meaning given to it by s 1 of the Mental Health Act 1983. The Mental Health Act defines mental disorder as: 'Mental illness, arrested or incomplete development of mind, psychopathic disorder and any other disorder of disability of mind'.

The offences set out in ss 30 to 33 of the SOA 2003 are only complete where it can be proved that the alleged offender knew or could reasonably be expected to have known that the person has a mental disorder and that because of it, or for a reason related to it, they were likely to be unable to refuse.

3.11.1 Section 30 Sexual activity with a person with a mental disorder impeding choice

A person commits an offence if he or she intentionally touches a person with a mental disorder impeding choice and the touching is sexual.

3.11.2 Section 31 Causing or inciting a person, with a mental disorder impeding choice, to engage in sexual activity

A person commits an offence if he or she intentionally causes or incites a person with a mental disorder impeding choice to engage in a sexual activity.

3.11.3 Section 32 Engaging in sexual activity in the presence of a person with a mental disorder impeding choice

A person commits an offence if he or she intentionally engages in a sexual activity and, for the purpose of obtaining sexual gratification, does so:

(a) When a person with a mental disorder impeding choice is either present or is in a place from which the sexual activity can be observed;
(b) In the knowledge, belief or intention that the person with a mental disorder impeding choice is aware of it.

3.11.4 Section 33 Causing a person, with a mental disorder impeding choice, to watch a sexual act

A person commits an offence if, for the purpose of obtaining sexual gratification, he or she intentionally causes a person with a mental disorder impeding choice to watch a third person engaging in a sexual activity or to look at an image of a person engaging in a sexual activity.

3.12 Inducements, etc to People with a Mental Disorder

The offences set out in ss 34 to 37 of the SOA 2003 relate to sexual activity with a person with a mental disorder where agreement to the behaviour is obtained by an inducement, threat, or deception.

These offences are only complete where it can be proved that the alleged offender knew or could reasonably be expected to have known that the person has a mental disorder.

3.12.1 Section 34 Inducement, threat, or deception to procure sexual activity with a person with a mental disorder

A person commits an offence if with an agreement obtained by means of an inducement, threat, or deception from a person with a mental disorder he or she intentionally touches that person and the touching is sexual.

3.12.2 Section 35 Causing a person with a mental disorder to engage in or agree to engage in sexual activity by inducement, threat, or deception

A person commits an offence if with an agreement obtained by means of an inducement, threat, or deception from a person with a mental disorder he or she intentionally causes that person to engage in, or to agree to engage in, a sexual activity.

3.12.3 Section 36 Engaging in sexual activity in the presence, procured by inducement, threat, or deception, of a person with a mental disorder

A person commits an offence if with an agreement obtained by means of an inducement, threat, or deception from a person with a mental disorder he or she intentionally engages in a sexual activity and, for the purpose of obtaining sexual gratification, does so:

(a) When the person with a mental disorder is either present or is in a place from which the sexual activity can be observed;
(b) In the knowledge, belief, or intention that the person with a mental disorder is aware of it.

3.12.4 Section 37 Causing a person with a mental disorder to watch a sexual act by inducement, threat, or deception

A person commits an offence if with an agreement obtained by means of an inducement, threat, or deception from a person with a mental disorder and for the purpose of obtaining sexual gratification, he or she intentionally causes the person with a mental disorder to watch a third person engaging in a sexual activity or to look at an image of a person engaging in a sexual activity.

3.13 Sexual Offences Committed by Care Workers Against People with a Mental Disorder

The sexual offences committed by care workers against people with a mental disorder that are set out in ss 38 to 41 of the SOA 2003 mirror those of an abuse of trust in relation to children in institutional settings.

The term 'care worker' is fairly wide ranging and is described in detail in s 42 of the SOA 2003. Briefly, it includes settings in which the offender looks after the person with a mental disorder in a:

- Care home;
- Community home;
- Voluntary home;
- Children's home; or
- Hospital or clinic (including private hospital or clinic).

It also includes circumstances in which the alleged offender is otherwise employed by:

- The National Health Service,
- An independent medical agency; or
- Any other provider of care assistance or services;

and has in the course of their employment regular face-to-face contact with the person with a mental disorder.

Exemptions from the offences set out in ss 38 to 41 exist where the parties concerned are lawfully married or had a lawful sexual relationship pre-dating the care relationship (ss 43 and 44).

The offences set out in ss 38 to 41 are only complete where it can be proved that the alleged offender knew or could reasonably be expected to have known that the person has a mental disorder.

3.13.1 Section 38 Care workers: sexual activity with a person with a mental disorder

A care worker commits an offence if he or she intentionally touches a person with a mental disorder and the touching is sexual.

3.13.2 Section 39 Care workers: causing or inciting sexual activity

A care worker commits an offence if he or she intentionally causes or incites a person with a mental disorder to engage in a sexual activity.

3.13.3 Section 40 Care workers: sexual activity in the presence of a person with a mental disorder

A care worker commits an offence if he or she intentionally engages in a sexual activity and, for the purpose of obtaining sexual gratification, does so:

(a) When a person with a mental disorder is either present or is in a place from which the sexual activity can be observed;
(b) In the knowledge, belief, or intention that the person with a mental disorder is aware of it.

3.13.4 **Section 41 Care workers: causing a person with a mental disorder to watch a sexual act**

A care worker commits an offence if, for the purpose of obtaining sexual gratification, he or she intentionally causes a person with a mental disorder to watch a third person engaging in a sexual activity or to look at an image of a person engaging in a sexual activity.

3.14 **Violent Offences (Including Cruelty)**

With the exception of common assault and battery, all the offences referred to in this section can be tried in the Crown Court: some can only be tried in the Crown Court while others can be tried either in the Magistrates' or the Crown Court, depending on the circumstances. Common assault and battery can only be tried in the Magistrates' Court.

3.14.1 **Homicide**

Two of the homicide offences mentioned in this book, murder and manslaughter, are offences under common law. The other homicide offence, infanticide, is contrary to the Infanticide Act 1938. For the sake of completeness, the offence of threats to kill under the Offences Against the Person Act 1861 is also mentioned.

Murder

'Murder is when a person unlawfully kills another human being under the Queen's peace and with malice aforethought' (Murphy, 1998). Malice aforethought refers to the intention to kill or cause grievous bodily harm.

Manslaughter

Manslaughter can be either voluntary or involuntary.

Voluntary manslaughter is committed when an unlawful killing occurs in circumstances where the alleged offender's intention to kill or cause grievous bodily harm is mitigated by provocation, diminished responsibility, or a suicide pact.

Involuntary manslaughter is committed when an unlawful homicide takes place in the absence of an intention to kill or cause grievous bodily harm.

Infanticide

Section 1 of the Infanticide Act 1938 states that a woman commits an offence if by a wilful act or omission she causes the death of her child when the child is under 12 months old and at a time when the balance of her mind is disturbed as a result of not having recovered from the birth of her child.

Threats to Kill

Section 16 of the Offences Against the Person Act 1861 states that a person commits an offence if, without a lawful excuse, he or she makes a threat to another person to kill them or somebody else.

3.14.2 **Assaults**

The offences of assault set out in this section vary in terms of their severity and of the alleged offender's intent in perpetrating them.

Section 18 of the Offences Against the Person Act 1861: grievous bodily harm or wounding with intent

A person commits an offence if he or she unlawfully and maliciously wounds or causes grievous bodily harm to another with the intention of causing grievous bodily harm; or resisting or preventing the lawful arrest or detention of any person.

A person acts 'maliciously' if they either intend to cause harm; or behave recklessly, after having foreseen the potential that their actions have to cause harm.

'Wound' means a break in the continuity of the whole skin (an internal rupturing of the blood vessels does not amount to a wound). 'Grievous bodily harm' means really serious harm.

Section 20 of the Offences Against the Person Act 1861: grievous bodily harm or wounding

A person commits an offence if he or she unlawfully and maliciously wounds or inflicts grievous bodily harm to another.

Section 47 of the Offences Against the Person Act 1861: assault occasioning actual bodily harm

A person commits an offence if he or she assaults a person occasioning them actual bodily harm. An 'assault' includes the use of physical violence or the threat of immediate unlawful physical violence. 'Actual bodily harm' means some form of hurt or injury calculated to interfere with the health or comfort of another. It does not have to be permanent but must be more than merely transient or trifling.

Section 39 of the Criminal Justice Act 1988: common assault and battery

A person commits an offence if he or she assaults a person.

3.15 Offences of Cruelty and Neglect

3.15.1 Section 1 of the Children and Young Persons Act 1933: Cruelty to Children

A person who is 16 or over and responsible for a child or young person under that age commits an offence if he or she wilfully:

- Assaults or causes or procures that child or young person to be assaulted;
- Ill-treats or causes or procures that child or young person to be ill-treated;
- Neglects or causes or procures that child or young person to be neglected;
- Abandons or causes or procures that child or young person to be abandoned;
- Exposes or causes or procures that child or young person to be exposed;

in a manner likely to cause the child unnecessary suffering or injury to health.

3.15.2 Section 44 of the Mental Capacity Act 2005: ill-treatment or neglect

A person commits an offence if he or she ill-treats or wilfully neglects another person who they care for that has a lack of capacity or who they reasonably believe to lack capacity.

This offence can also be committed where the alleged offender has a power of attorney in respect of the person who lacks capacity or is a deputy appointed by a court for the person who lacks capacity.

3.16 Chapter Summary

This chapter has outlined the offences of most concern to those involved in the investigation of offences involving vulnerable people as victims of crime. To this end it has focused on sexual and violent offences, including cruelty and neglect.

SPACE FOR NOTES

SPACE FOR NOTES

SPACE FOR NOTES

Human Trafficking

4.1 **Introduction**

Trafficking can be equated with slavery. International law prohibits slavery and the slave trade, and the prohibition on slavery is part of customary international law. This means that it applies to all States irrespective of whether they have ratified the various international treaties which prohibit slavery (such as the Slavery Conventions and the International Covenant on Civil and Political Rights).

In February 1806, Lord Grenville made a passionate speech in the House of Lords where he argued that the slave trade was 'contrary to the principles of justice, humanity and sound policy' and criticized fellow members for 'not having abolished the trade long ago'. The Abolition of the Slave Trade bill was passed in the House of Lords and became law on 25 March 1807. However, it was not until 1833 that Parliament passed the Slave Abolition Act. This Act gave all slaves in the British Empire their freedom.

Violence, coercion, and deception are used to take people away from their families and force them to work against their will. People are trafficked both between countries and internally within their own country. People who are subjected to trafficking will be forced to work as domestics, labourers, factory workers, and into prostitution.

People will in some cases put themselves or their children in the hands of traffickers in a bid to escape poverty, discrimination, or civil war. They are promised fantastic opportunities such as well-paid jobs, a good education, or marriage. Many are told that they will be able to send money home for food to help to pay for travel for the rest of the family.

4.2 **How Does Trafficking Occur?**

Many people who are looking to migrate in search of work are faced by complex and restrictive immigration laws. They therefore often have to resort to relying upon other agencies or friends of friends to help them with their travel plans. If they are lucky, the agency or persons that they contact, or are put into contact with, will be honest and assist them with their plans, however if they are not honest then they will find themselves in the hands of a trafficker whose only interest is financial gain. This trafficker will then isolate them, before exploiting them to make money from them.

Traffickers usually target people who are in desperate need of money. Families or individuals are approached directly by the traffickers with promises of well-paid work, money, or even of further education or schooling.

Sometimes people are recruited through agencies that offer to make all the travel arrangements and help the victim acquire all the necessary travel documentation, with the promise of a 'well-paid job' when they arrive at their destination.

The trafficker may also offer to cover all the travel and accommodation expenses in the form of a loan, telling the person that they can repay the debt once they start their new job.

However, a system of debt bondage soon starts to emerge. Once the victim has arrived at their final destination, they will discover that the promise of employment was false and in reality never did exist. The victim will also find that they still have to pay back the loan that the trafficker gave them to pay for the cost of the travel expenses. They will discover that the loan will then be vastly inflated through interest on the money 'borrowed', and they will be charged an extortionate amount of money for accommodation and food.

If the victim is given the opportunity to work, they will find that they are only paid a small percentage of the wage that they were promised at the start; in some cases they will receive nothing at all. In this scenario it will be impossible for the victim to pay back the original loan amount or pay future food and accommodation charges.

To prevent the victim from attempting to gain accommodation or employment that is not provided by the traffickers, any travel documents and/or passports will be retained by the traffickers. Stories of police cruelty, harassment, arrest, and deportation will be told by the traffickers to ensure that victims are too afraid to tell anyone or try to escape.

The trafficker will also keep a tight hold on the victim through the use of threats of rape, torture, violence, and intimidation. Threats could also be made towards family and friends who remain at home in order to get the victim to comply with the demands made by traffickers.

4.3 **The Palermo Protocol**

On 15 November 2000, the United Nations General Assembly adopted the United Nations Convention against Transnational Organized Crime.

This Convention calls upon countries to take measures against organized crime and to co-operate with each other. The Convention came into force on 23 September 2003 and the United Kingdom is a signatory. Article 25 of the Convention states that each country shall take appropriate measures within its means to provide assistance and protection to victims of offences covered by the Convention.

To supplement this Convention, there is also a protocol that supports the fight against sex trafficking. As this Protocol was signed in Palermo, Italy, it is widely known as and referred to as the 'Palermo Protocol'. Its correct title, however, is a little lengthier as follows: 'Protocol to Prevent, Suppress and Punish Trafficking in Persons, especially Women and Children, supplementing the United Nations Convention Against Trans-national Organised Crime.'

The Palermo Protocol was adopted by resolution A/RES/55/25 of 15 November 2000 at the 55th session of the General Assembly of the United Nations. The

United Kingdom became a signatory to the Protocol on 14 December 2000 at the Palazzi di Giustizia in Palermo, Italy. The Protocol came into force on 25 December 2003 and was ratified by the United Kingdom on 9 February 2006.

This Protocol can be broken down into three interdependent elements that must all be present to constitute a breach of Article 3:

- Movement—the recruitment, transportation, transfer, harbouring, or receiving of persons;
- Means of securing movement—the threat or use of force or other forms of coercion, abduction, fraud, deception, abuse of power or a position of vulnerability, or the giving or receiving of payments or benefits to achieve the consent of a person having control over another person;
- Purpose of movement—to exploit the person in the ways listed in the Article.

Each of the three elements must be present together to breach the Protocol; the action must be achieved by one of the means and both must be aimed at achieving the exploitative purpose. If any one of the three elements is missing, the necessary conditions for a crime of trafficking as determined by Article 3 of the Palermo Protocol have not been met.

The only exception to this is when the situation involves a person under the age of 18 years. In such cases, it is only necessary to show the movement and that this was for purposes of exploitation. In the case of children, it is sufficient to breach the Protocol if only the activity and exploitative purpose are present—the means by which it is achieved is disregarded.

4.4 The Sexual Offences Act 2003

As well as the international conventions that deal with offences relating to the crime of trafficking in human beings, there are several new offences in UK law that have been created under the Sexual Offences Act 2003 that specifically deal with the issue of human trafficking and help to redress the situation that investigators find themselves in when dealing with human trafficking.

4.4.1 Section 57 Trafficking into the UK for sexual exploitation

(1) A person commits an offence if he intentionally arranges or facilitates the arrival in the United Kingdom of another person (B) and either—
    (a) he intends to do anything to or in respect of B, after B's arrival but in any part of the world, which if done will involve the commission of a relevant offence, or
    (b) he believes that another person is likely to do something to or in respect of B, after B's arrival but in any part of the world, which if done will involve the commission of a relevant offence.

(2) A person guilty of an offence under this section is liable—
- (a) on summary conviction, to imprisonment for a term not exceeding 6 months or a fine not exceeding the statutory maximum or both;
- (b) on conviction on indictment, to imprisonment for a term not exceeding 14 years.

4.4.2 Section 58 Trafficking within the UK for sexual exploitation

(1) A person commits an offence if he intentionally arranges or facilitates travel within the United Kingdom by another person (B) and either—
- (a) he intends to do anything to or in respect of B, during or after the journey and in any part of the world, which if done will involve the commission of a relevant offence, or
- (b) he believes that another person is likely to do something to or in respect of B, during or after the journey and in any part of the world, which if done will involve the commission of a relevant offence.

(2) A person guilty of an offence under this section is liable—
- (a) on summary conviction, to imprisonment for a term not exceeding 6 months or a fine not exceeding the statutory maximum or both
- (b) on conviction on indictment, to imprisonment for a term not exceeding 14 years

4.4.3 Section 59 Trafficking out of the UK for sexual exploitation

(1) A person commits an offence if he intentionally arranges or facilitates the departure from the United Kingdom of another person (B) and either—
- (a) he intends to do anything to or in respect of B, after B's departure but in any part of the world, which if done will involve the commission of a relevant offence, or
- (b) he believes that another person is likely to do something to or in respect of B, after B's departure but in any part of the world, which if done will involve the commission of a relevant offence.

(2) A person guilty of an offence under this section is liable—
- (a) on summary conviction, to imprisonment for a term not exceeding 6 months or a fine not exceeding the statutory maximum or both;
- (b) on conviction on indictment, to imprisonment for a term not exceeding 14 years.

4.5 Migrant Smuggling

For the first time, migrant smuggling has been defined by the international community, in an instrument which was adopted at the same time as the Palermo Protocol.

Article 3 of the Protocol against the Smuggling of Migrants by Land, Sea and Air, supplementing the United Nations Convention against Transnational Organized Crime defines migrant smuggling as follows:

Definition of migrant smuggling

Smuggling of migrants means the procurement, in order to obtain, directly or indirectly, a financial or other material benefit, of the illegal entry of a person into a State Party of which the person is not a national or a permanent resident.

This definition also contains several elements which must be separately shown to exist:

- There must be movement and this movement must be across an international border;
- The cross-border movement which is being facilitated must be illegal;
- The purpose of the facilitated movement must be profit.

4.6 How Are Trafficked People Controlled?

The fundamental aim of traffickers is to earn money or receive services through the long-term exploitation of their victims. This means that they will need to ensure that the victim will continue to work as instructed and not try to escape. To be able to do this, the traffickers needs to maintain a continuous control over their victims.

Regardless of the exploitative purpose, there are many different measures that are used to control the victims of trafficking during the exploitation phase. Each measure may be used in isolation, or as part of a combined package of measures. In most instances, measures will be combined so as to create an environment of actual or psychological imprisonment of the victim.

One of the primary measures of control is debt bondage in which the victim is required to repay the exorbitant costs that were allegedly incurred for bringing the trafficked person to the final destination point. This control measure occurs mainly in sex exploitation cases, but can be utilized in labour exploitation cases. In sexual exploitation cases, exorbitant interest rates are often applied to the original costs which are again inflated by the requirement to pay vastly inflated prices for residential or brothel accommodation, resulting in an ever-mounting debt bond that becomes effectively impossible to pay off.

In cases involving transportation that requires the use of identity and or travel documents, traffickers may remove the documents immediately after the victim arrives at their final destination. This means that the victim has no official identity; this will tend to confirm their illegal entry status and makes it very difficult for them to seek help or to escape without the risk of detention and/or punishment.

Traffickers will whenever possible reinforce the victim's fear of the police and authorities by telling the victim either that she or he is free to leave and go to the police if they wish, but that the outcome will be immediate deportation, and that reprisals will be inflicted as a consequence.

This fear of the police or other forms of authority, often combined with the lack of documentation, is exploited by the traffickers in order to make it highly unlikely that trafficked victims will attempt to affect an escape or to make any complaints against their traffickers.

Traffickers make full use of violence and the threat of violence as an effective means of control. Physical abuse may be inflicted as punishment for disobedience and will be designed to serve as a warning to ensure compliance and that victims are fully aware of the consequences of transgressing.

The most effective threat is the threat of reprisals against loved ones of the victim who remain in the country of origin. In many cases, the traffickers will already know the victim's family background and know a range of details of the victim's family circumstances. The problem for the victim is that they cannot afford to take risks with the safety of their loved ones.

Why do not more victims escape from their traffickers? The answer to this question lies in the ability to collectively consider all of the control measures and to then view the situation from the prospect of the victim and consider their position against the whole range of measures. When all of these factors are considered, it becomes easier to understand why so few trafficked victims seek to escape from their traffickers.

Child trafficking generally involves the making of a financial incentive to a parent or guardian in order to gain their co-operation. This is nearly always accompanied by a degree of deception regarding the nature of the child's future employment or position.

4.7 **Chapter Summary**

This chapter has considered the issue of trafficking and migrant smuggling. It has set out the ways in which trafficked people are often controlled in the hope of informing those involved in investigating offences of this nature.

The fact that slavery—in the form of human trafficking—still exists in the 21st century is a shameful reflection on society. The trafficking in human beings can under certain circumstances be equated with slavery. There are international conventions and Laws, which prohibit the actions of persons connected with slavery and the slave trade.

In 1948, the Universal Declaration of Human Rights proclaimed that, 'no-one shall be held in slavery and servitude'. Over 50 years later, the problems associated with slavery and of slave labour remain unresolved. These issues have in fact extended and evolved beyond their historical background, as the reality of the trade and movement of children and adults alike remains unchanged.

It is only more recently that treaties and conventions have been developed, and a separate international legal regime has gradually emerged (such as the Slavery Conventions and the International Covenant on Civil and Political Rights).

SPACE FOR NOTES

SPACE FOR NOTES

SPACE FOR NOTES

5

Multi-Agency Working

5.1 **Introduction**

Multi-agency working and the sharing of investigatively important information between agencies is vital to the thorough and efficient investigation of crime.

The local authority or any other agencies or organizations who are charged with the care and protection of vulnerable persons should inform the police as soon as it becomes apparent, or it is suspected, that a criminal offence has been committed, or if a course of conduct has been pursued by any person that could place a vulnerable person at risk or in danger. This does not mean that every time that the police are informed of an incident involving a child or vulnerable adult, there will be a criminal investigation or further police involvement. It is vitally important, however, that the police remain involved and retain the opportunity to be informed and consulted, to ensure all relevant information can be taken into account before any final decision is made.

The police should, wherever possible, work jointly with social services and in partnership with any other agencies, but they will retain the responsibility to instigate and conduct all investigations into criminal matters, they should always maintain a close working relationship with and consider any views expressed by other agencies.

5.2 **Joint Working**

The police need (where relevant) to work jointly with social services to establish the facts about any offence or offences which may have been committed against a child, and to collect evidence relating to any offences under investigation in a professional and proper manner.

Part of the work conducted by the social services/police joint investigation team may entail the conducting of an assessment into the needs of a child and of the capacity of the child's parents and family network to appropriately ensure the child's safety. The joint investigation team will obtain information (usually in the form of interviews) from numerous persons and sources to effectively build up a picture of the child's current situation or circumstances leading up to the situation under investigation. This may also include interviews with other professionals and/or persons who are connected with the subject and medical examinations where appropriate. A joint police/social services investigation team may on occasion need to speak to a child victim without the knowledge of the parent or guardian, and it is important for investigators to remember that any such investigations should be carried out in a thoroughly professional and sensitive manner.

Any evidence that is gathered during the process of a criminal investigation may also be of use to local authority solicitors who may be considering taking out care or civil proceedings in the High Court. On occasion the police solicitors department or Crown Prosecution Service (CPS) will need to be consulted prior to any information being passed or exchanged, in the normal series of events any evidence will normally be shared if it is not considered to be subject to subjudice or the disclosure of such information would be detrimental to any criminal proceedings currently under investigation.

The evidential standards required by the criminal and civil courts differ significantly. The burden of proof required by a criminal court is referred to as being proof that is 'beyond reasonable doubt'. It is also for the prosecution to prove that the defendant committed the act or acts that they are accused of committing, and not for the defendant to prove their innocence. Whereas for proceedings held in the civil court, the standard of proof that is required is much lower and is decided on the 'balance of probabilities'.

It is not unusual for the police or the CPS to come to the conclusion that criminal proceedings cannot be instigated against a person suspected of committing offences against a vulnerable person on the grounds that there is insufficient evidence to meet the higher standard of proof, while a civil court is still able to decide that the vulnerable person needs protection from that same suspect.

It is also important for investigators to remember that while the criminal courts focus on the guilt and behaviour of the defendant, the focus of the civil courts is directed more towards the best interests of the child.

In addition to their duty to investigate criminal offences the police have emergency powers to enter premises and ensure the immediate protection of children believed to be suffering from, or at risk of, significant harm. Such powers should be used only as a last resort and in any event in an emergency, the principle being that wherever possible the decision to remove a child from a parent or carer should be planned with the ultimate decision being made by the civil court.

5.3 **Child Protection Cases**

The objective of any inquiries conducted under s 47 of the Children Act 1989 is to determine whether any action is needed by agencies to promote and safeguard the welfare of any child or children who are the subject of that inquiry. The social services department should decide how to proceed following s 47 inquiries, after discussion between all those who have conducted or been significantly involved in those inquiries, including relevant professionals and agencies, as well as foster carers where involved, and the child and parents themselves.

The outcome of s 47 inquiries should be recorded and parents (together with professionals and agencies who have been significantly involved) should receive a copy of this record, in particular in advance of any initial child conference that is convened. It may be valuable, following an evaluation of the outcome of inquiries, to make recommendations for action in an inter-disciplinary forum, if the case is not going forward to a child protection conference.

Following the inquiry into the death of Victoria Climbié, Lord Lamming made numerous recommendations, perhaps one of the most controversial recommendations that would potentially impact on multi-agency working was one that was made in respect of the police. Recommendation 99 states:

> The *Working Together* arrangements must be amended to ensure the police carry out completely, and exclusively, any criminal investigation elements in a case of suspected injury or harm to a child, including the evidential interview with a child victim. This will remove any confusion about which agency takes the 'lead' or is responsible for certain actions. (para 14.57)

This recommendation while attempting to ensure that any investigation is carried out thoroughly and completely could prove problematic when conducting joint investigations if an extreme interpretation is adopted. For this reason, the revised edition of *Achieving Best Evidence in Criminal Proceedings* (Home Office, 2007) says:

> Where it has been agreed by the police and the local children's services authority, in a strategy discussion/meeting, that it is in the best interests of the child that a full criminal investigation be carried out, the police are responsible for that investigation, including any investigative interview (video-recorded or otherwise) with the victim (recommendation 99 of the Victoria Climbié Inquiry Report). Having responsibility for the criminal investigation does not mean that the police should always take the lead in the investigative interview. Provided both the police officer and children's social care social worker have been adequately trained to interview child witnesses in accordance with the guidance set out in this document, there is no reason why either should not lead the interview. The decision as to who leads the interview should depend on who is able to establish the best rapport with the child. In circumstances where a children's social care social worker leads the interview, the police should retain their responsibility for the criminal investigation by ensuring that the interview is properly planned and that the police officer has an effective role in monitoring the interview [...]. Similarly, where a police officer leads the interview, the local authority should retain their duty to investigate under Section 47 of the Children Act 1989 by ensuring that the interview is properly planned and that the children's social care social worker has an effective role in monitoring the interview (para 2.12).

5.4 Vulnerable Adult Abuse

Any person working for or involved with vulnerable adults should be vigilant to the possibility of abuse. To this end, it is the responsibility of all staff to act on any suspicion or evidence of abuse or neglect and to pass on their concerns to a responsible person or agency.

When dealing with vulnerable adults it is important for investigators to appreciate that any initial actions taken may need to be primarily supportive in order to gain the trust and confidence of such witnesses.

Disclosures of alleged abuse may come from a variety of sources. The disclosure may, for example, be raised by the victim, a concerned relative, or a carer or other professional. It may be given as a direct disclosure, or it may come to light during an assessment or medical intervention. On occasion the matter may be reported directly to the police, especially if the matter is very serious.

Anonymous information must be handled with the greatest of care and with sensitivity. In such cases the early involvement of the police may have benefits. In particular:

- To establish whether a criminal act or acts have been committed;
- To help ensure that forensic evidence is not lost or contaminated;
- Police officers have considerable skill in investigating and interviewing.

The communication needs of victims including people with sensory impairments, learning disabilities, dementia, or whose first language is not English must be taken into account. Interviewers and interpreters will require specialist training.

There has to be agreed protocols to deal with responsibilities, specific tasks, and the best use of the skills available. However, it needs to be remembered that no individual agency's statutory responsibility can be delegated to another. Each individual agency must act in accordance with its own duty and guidelines, and only take appropriate action after due consideration has been given to the outcome of such action and its impact on the child or vulnerable adult concerned. Any and all information received must be constantly evaluated and reviewed by each individual agency concerned.

Whenever an allegation or disclosure of abuse of any kind is made all agencies should keep clear and accurate records of the disclosure or allegation made. If it is assessed that an individual continues to pose a threat to other service users then this information must be shared with other agencies in order that appropriate action can be taken to protect other vulnerable persons.

Once the initial facts of the allegation or disclosure have been established, an assessment of the needs of the victim will need to be made. This will entail a strategy discussion or meeting. This will need to encompass such things as decisions about planning for the person's future protection. In making decisions about what is the most appropriate action to take, the rights of an adult or older child to make choices and take risks and of their capacity to make decisions about the way in which an investigation is conducted or of the management of the abusive situation should be taken into account. It will not however limit the action that may be required to be taken.

Making sure that vulnerable adults, who need care and support, are in safe hands is one of the key principles of the White Paper, *Building for the Future*. The intention of this proposal is to improve the regulation of social services and to raise standards in the workforce. This is being taken forward through the Care Standards Bill, and identifies the protection and promotion of the welfare of vulnerable adults as a priority. This guidance reinforces the concept of the respect for a person's human rights contained in the provisions of the Human Rights Act 1998.

This guidance also addresses the need for the development of local multi-agency codes of practice that are based on a consistent framework for the protection of vulnerable adults.

Any local policies developed by social services departments should take account of the measures to provide greater protection to vulnerable or intimidated witnesses in the criminal justice system, as recommended in *Speaking Up for Justice* (Home Office, 1998).

The multi-agency guidance set out in *No Secrets* and *In Safe Hands* (see Chapter 2) define an adult as somebody who is over 18. Both documents then go on to take their definition of a vulnerable adult from the Law Commission (1997) report 'Who Decides? Making Decisions on Behalf of Mentally Incapacitated Adults'. This definition provides a basis from which to develop practice and is as follows:

Definition of Vulnerable Adult

A vulnerable adult is a person 'who is or may be in need of community care services by reason of mental or other disability, age or illness and who is or may be unable to take care of himself or herself, or unable to protect himself or herself against significant harm or serious exploitation'.

Law Commission (1997)

The kind of abuse covered in *No Secrets* and *In Safe Hands* is wide ranging and includes:

- Physical abuse, including hitting, slapping, beating, over-medication, or misuse of a person's medication, undue restraint, or inappropriate sanctions;
- Sexual abuse, including sexual acts or sexual intercourse (rape) to which the vulnerable adult was pressured into, or was incapable of giving consent;
- Psychological abuse including threats, humiliation, verbal/racial abuse, isolation;
- Financial abuse including theft, fraud, misuse, or misappropriation of benefits;
- Neglect, including failure to access medical care or services, negligence in the face of risk-taking, failure to give prescribed medication, poor nutrition, or lack of or failure to provide for a person's basic needs.

Vulnerable adults are entitled to the same level of protection from the law as other people. In addition to this expectation, certain statutory offences have been created which specifically protect those people who are unable to protect themselves or may be incapacitated in any way.

When complaints about alleged or suspected abuse suggest that a criminal offence has or may have been committed it is absolutely imperative that the matter should be referred to the police as a matter of urgency. Criminal investigations conducted by the police will always take priority over all other lines of inquiry by other agencies.

The seriousness or extent of abuse is often not clear when a concern is first raised so it is important to approach allegations or concerns with an open mind about the appropriateness of intervention. However, a referral should still be made to one of the statutory agencies without delay in all cases.

Factors relevant in any assessment of seriousness should include:

- The frailty, age, or vulnerability of the person involved;
- The extent of any harm;
- The frequency or length of time that the abuse has occurred;
- The impact of the abuse on the individual person.

The Law Commission makes use of the concept of significant harm as an important threshold when considering the nature of intervention by which they mean:

> ill treatment (including sexual abuse and forms of ill treatment that are not physical); the impairment of, or an avoidable deterioration in physical or mental health; and the impairment of physical, emotional, social or behavioural development. (Law Commission Report 1995, p 207).

Significant harm may comprise of a single event which, when regarded in isolation, may seem insignificant but as part of a series of incidents which may be more serious if it occurs.

5.5 **Chapter Summary**

This chapter has discussed multi-agency working in the context of offences against children and offences against vulnerable adults.

There is no doubt that the advantages to be found in developing good working practices with partner agencies can enhance any investigative process. Each individual organization will always retain responsibility for its own actions and specific areas of accountability. However, the opportunity to appropriately exchange information and ideas at strategy meetings and to share ideas should not be dismissed out of hand simply because agencies are precious about their own information or do not wish to share ideas.

SPACE FOR NOTES

SPACE FOR NOTES

SPACE FOR NOTES

6

Special Measures

6.1 **Introduction**

The survey of vulnerable and intimidated witnesses reported by Hamlyn *et al* (2004) and the evaluation of the implementation of special measures reported by Burton *et al* (2006) both indicate that the use of special measures during a trial has benefits. Burton *et al* also report that only a minority of vulnerable and intimidated witnesses were identified as such by the police and that identification by the Crown Prosecution Service (CPS) was rare when the police had not already done so. In these circumstances, the identification of witnesses as vulnerable or intimidated was largely left to the Witness Service, giving rise to a situation in which many applications for special measures were either not made until the trial commenced or were not made at all. This situation is at odds with the recommendation originally made in *Speaking Up for Justice* that the police should be the agency to obtain the views of vulnerable and intimidated witnesses about which of the available special measures should be applied for (Recommendation 24). Such a state of affairs is no longer tenable because it amounts to a contravention of the *Code of Practice for Victims of Crime* (Office for Criminal Justice Reform, 2005).

The *Code of Practice for Victims of Crime* places a responsibility on the police to identify vulnerable and intimidated victims (para 5.7) and to explain special measures to them when the information that they have is such that they might be called to give evidence in court (para 5.8). Such a responsibility is echoed in respect of witnesses more generally in Charter Standard 3 of the consultation draft of the *Witness Charter* (Office for Criminal Justice Reform, 2005). *Victim and Witness Delivery Toolkit 5* (Office for Criminal Justice Reform, 2005) also makes it clear that it is the responsibility of the police to 'provide witnesses with clear explanations of the special measures that may be available to them and how these work in practice' (p 8). It is also consistent with the Youth Justice and Criminal Evidence Act (YJCEA) because it obliges the court to take account of the witness's views in the context of all the circumstances of the case, including the ability of the parties involved to test the evidence, when considering whether special measures are likely to maximize the quality of the witness's evidence (s 19(3)(a)). The important point here is that special measures should be explained to witnesses so that they can make informed judgments about them. This clearly goes beyond simply listing the special measures and into the realm of entering into a dialogue with the witness during which an adequate and accurate description of the various measures are provided together with an account of their benefits and limitations. The purpose of this chapter is to equip practitioners working in the Criminal Justice System with the information necessary to meet this responsibility.

6.2 **Special Measures**

The 'special measures' set out in Pt 2 of the YJCEA are:

- Screens;
- Live TV link;
- Evidence in private;
- Removal of wigs and gowns;
- Video-recorded evidence-in-chief;
- Video-recorded cross-examination;
- Intermediaries; and
- Communication aids.

Each of these measures will now be considered in detail.

6.2.1 **The use of screens (section 23 YJCEA)**

Description

Screens or curtains (depending on the layout of the court) are positioned around the witness box so as to prevent the defendant from seeing the witness and the witness from seeing the defendant. The witness will still be able to see and be seen by the judge or magistrate, at least one legal representative of the prosecution and defence and, if the case is being heard in the Crown Court, the jury.

Benefits

- The impact of the defendant's presence on the witness is minimized by virtue of them being out of sight.
- The witness is not exposed to the defendant's non-verbal reactions.

Limitations

The defendant can still hear the witness and might, therefore, recognize their voice. This might be a problem where there are witness intimidation issues and the defendant is unaware of the witness's identity.

6.2.2 **The use of live TV link (section 24 YJCEA)**

Description

The witness gives live evidence from a room outside the courtroom (usually, though not always, located in the court building). The witness's testimony is relayed live into the courtroom via TV link.

Benefits

- The impact of the defendant's presence on the witness is minimized by virtue of them being out of sight.

- The witness is not exposed to the defendant's non-verbal reactions.
- The witness gives evidence in a less intimidating environment than the court-room.

Limitations

The defendant will see the witness on live TV screen and, therefore, might recognize them. This might be a problem where there are witness intimidation issues and the defendant is unaware of the witness's identity.

6.2.3 **Giving evidence in private (section 25 YJCEA)**

Description

Members of the public are excluded from the court while the witness is giving evidence. Only one nominated member of the media is allowed to be present. This is predominantly for use in sexual offence cases and in some cases of intimidation.

Benefits

- Has the potential to reduce the embarrassment likely to be experienced by the witness when giving sensitive evidence.
- The witness might feel less intimidated than he or she would if the defendant's family or associates were present in the public gallery.

Limitations

Members of the witness's family or associates who might lend emotional support are also excluded from the public gallery while the witness is giving evidence.

6.2.4 **The removal of wigs and gowns (section 26 YJCEA)**

Description

The judge and lawyers remove their wigs and gowns.

Benefits

The removal of wigs and gowns might serve to reduce the formality of the situation in court leading to a reduction in the anxiety experienced by the witness.

Limitations

The witness might prefer the formality of the situation enhanced by wigs and gowns, wanting 'their day in a proper court'.

6.2.5 The use of video-recorded interviews as evidence-in-chief (section 27 YJCEA)

Description

The video-recorded interview conducted during the investigation is played as the witness's evidence-in-chief.

Benefits

The witness does not have to repeat what was said during the police interview.

Limitations

- The defendant will see the video recording as part of pre-trial defence preparation and when it is played in court. This might be a problem where there are witness intimidation issues and the defendant is unaware of the witness' identity.
- The witness still has to go to court for cross-examination (other than in the very exceptional circumstances set out in s 116 of the Criminal Justice Act 2003), although such cross-examination usually takes place on live TV link.

6.2.6 The use of video-recorded cross-examination (section 28 YJCEA)

The implementation of video-recorded cross-examination has been delayed pending the publication of the Child Evidence Review by the Home Office and the views of ministers about its recommendations. For this reason, it is uncertain how this measure will work in practice or the extent to which it will be implemented.

6.2.7 Communication through intermediaries (section 29 YJCEA)

Description

Communication is either mediated by or takes place through an intermediary. Intermediaries are specialists in the use of idiosyncratic methods of communication, including sign and symbol systems. In common with interpreters, they can be used during a police witness interview and in court. However, their role goes beyond that of an interpreter in that they can 'explain' questions put to the witness and any replies given by the witness.

Benefits

Witnesses whose communications might have previously been either misunderstood, misrepresented, or ignored by those involved in the investigative or trial processes can be given the assistance that they might need to communicate more effectively in the Criminal Justice System. This should make the administration of justice more effective by reducing the confusion sometimes experienced by the witness, investigators, the courts, and lawyers. It should also open up access to justice to some of those who were previously denied it.

Limitations

A third party is involved in the process of communication.

6.2.8 The use of special communication aids (section 30 YJCEA)

Description

Witness communicates via a 'device' (eg a computer) when giving evidence.

Benefits

Witnesses whose communications might have previously been disregarded by those involved in the Criminal Justice System can now use the aids that they use on an everyday basis or that they have recently been introduced to in order to help them communicate.

Limitations

Communication takes place on an indirect basis.

6.3 Access to Special Measures

Both the legislation and Burton *et al* suggest that access to special measures depends on a three stage test:

(1) Does the witness fit the definition of one who is vulnerable or intimidated? If so:
(2) Are special measures necessary to enable the witness to give his/her best evidence? If so:
(3) Which particular special measures are most likely to help the witness give his/her best evidence?

1. Does the witness fit the definition of one who is vulnerable or intimidated?

The issue here is primarily one of whether the witness falls within the scope of ss 16 or 17 of the YJCEA, the details of which have already been set out in Chapter 1 above. There are, however, a few additional points worth repeating here:

- All witnesses under 17 are automatically regarded as vulnerable by virtue of s 16(1)(a) of the YJCEA;
- Any consideration of whether an adult witness with a disorder or disability can be said to be eligible under section 16 of the YJCEA must take account of:
  - The witness' views about the nature and extent of the disorder or disability (eg some witnesses might not consider themselves as having a disability) (section 16(4));
  - The extent to which the witness's disorder or disability is one that is likely to have an adverse impact on the completeness, coherence, and accuracy of

their evidence (ie the extent to which the disorder or disability in question impacts on the witness' ability to communicate) (s 16(5)).

Witnesses will only be regarded as intimidated by virtue of s 17 of the YJCEA if their fear or distress is connected with testifying in the court proceedings that might follow on from an investigation.

For the most part, whether or not a witness can be regarded as intimidated depends on the court taking account of a number of factors specified in the legislation such as the type of offence, the witness's age, domestic circumstances, ethnic origins, and cultural background as well as the behaviour of the accused person and his/her associates (these factors are more fully described in Chapter 1 above). What follows from this is an interpretation in the various guidance documents that accompany the legislation of what the legal definition set out in s 17 might mean in practice. Such guidance (notably, *Achieving Best Evidence in Criminal Proceedings: Guidance for Vulnerable or Intimidated Witnesses, including Children* and *Vulnerable Witnesses: A Police Service Guide*) quite reasonably cites victims of and witnesses to offences such as domestic violence and racially aggravated offences as examples of witnesses who could be considered to be intimidated.

Complainants in cases of sexual assault are defined as falling into this category per se by s 17(4) of the YJCEA. The effect of this is that witnesses alleging that they are victims of a sexual assault automatically fall within the definition of intimidated, without the need for interpretation of the kind described above.

2. Are special measures necessary to enable the witness to give his/her best evidence?

This consideration is to do with whether special measures in general are necessary. According to Burton *et al*, in the case of vulnerability this is a question of the witness's capacity to give their best evidence without assistance. In the case of intimidation, this is a question of the witness's willingness to give their best evidence. When considering the capacity and willingness of the witness, it is important to take account of the additional stress likely to be experienced by the witness by the court situation (eg the mental condition of a witness with a disorder such as schizophrenia might deteriorate as a result of the additional stress of being required to give evidence, having an adverse impact on the effectiveness of their communication).

3. Which particular special measures are most likely to help the witness give his/her best evidence?

In determining which particular special measure is appropriate, the courts will take account of the circumstances of the case, including the views of the witness and the extent to which the measure being considered is likely to inhibit the testing of the evidence by any of the parties to the proceedings (s 19(3) of the YJCEA). In terms of investigative practice, the effect of this is that investigators will need to explain special measures as noted in the introduction to this chapter. Several important qualifications should, however, be made about this:

- There is little point in soliciting the views of a witness about any given special measure unless it is actually available to them. Availability depends on two factors: limitations specified in the legislation and limitations arising from the phased implementation timetable.

The legislation

Section 18(1) of the Act makes it clear that the special measures specified in ss 23 to 28 are applicable to both 'vulnerable' and 'intimidated' witnesses whereas the measures contained in ss 29 and 30 (intermediaries and special communication aids) are only applicable to 'vulnerable' witnesses.

The phased implementation timetable

The implementation timetable is a phased one that commenced on 24 July 2002. While implementation has steadily progressed since then, many special measures still await implementation. The implementation timetable is regularly updated by way of an attachment to a Home Office Circular advising practitioners in the Criminal Justice System that another provision has been implemented. These Home Office Circulars are published on the Home Office internet site and should be regularly accessed by investigators and trainers.

- While child witnesses in cases involving sexual or violent offences (children 'in need of special protection') are automatically entitled to give their evidence-in-chief by way of a pre-recorded video interview and to be cross-examined on live TV link, the consent of the witness is still required (and the witness's carers or guardians where appropriate, see the consent chapter in this book). The strong presumption suggested by s 21(5) of the YJCEA that children 'in need of special protection' will give their evidence by video and live TV link is, therefore, still constrained by the witness's views in the form of consent.
- Explanations to child witnesses will clearly need to take account of their age and understanding. Explanation to witnesses over 16 where mental ability might be an issue is covered by the Mental Capacity Act 2005 and its associated Code of Practice. The Act places an obligation on all those involved to adapt their language in such a way as to ensure that the information needed to make decisions of this nature is effectively communicated (s 3(2) of the Act and para 2.18 of the consultation draft Code). The Act also makes provisions for those who are considered, following assessment, not to have the capacity to make such decisions.
- In seeking the witness's views about these special measures, it is imperative that investigators do **not** give the impression that the CPS will automatically apply for them or that the court will automatically grant access to them. While the courts are obliged to take account of the views of the witness, the

decision about access to special measures very much depends on the particular merits of the case.

6.4 **Limits to Special Measures**

While special measures under the YJCEA will certainly maximize the quality of a vulnerable or intimidated witness's evidence in most cases, an application under the legislation will not meet all the witness's needs in every case. For example, no provision is made in the Act for the protection that might be afforded to a witness by editing the recording of an interview by means of pixilation or altering the pitch of the witness's voice; no provision is made for turning off the defendant's screen where evidence is given by live TV link; and no provision is made for referring to the witness by means of a pseudonym. Where it is considered that such measures might be necessary, the appropriate course of action would be for the police to discuss with the CPS the possibility of inviting the court to make use of its inherent common law powers to do what it considers necessary in the interests of justice (supported by a precedent set in case law or otherwise). Such a discussion between the police and the CPS should also form part of an early special measures meeting where the prospect of making an application under the YJCEA is being considered.

6.4.1 **Communication between the police and the Crown Prosecution Service**

The police should inform the CPS of the potential need to make an application for special measures on forms MG2, MG6, and MG11. In addition to this, an 'early special measures' meeting between the police and the CPS will often be appropriate. Practice guidance in relation to early special measures meetings is set out in *Early Special Measures Meetings between the Police and the Crown Prosecution Service and between the Crown Prosecution Service and Vulnerable or Intimidated Witnesses* (Home Office, 2001). Such meetings are a valuable opportunity to discuss potential applications for special measures and the agreements reached during them can influence decision-making about some investigative procedures (eg the use of an intermediary, video-recording the interview) and the willingness of the witness to participate in the criminal justice process (as might be the case with the use of screens or live TV link).

Several points are worth emphasizing in the practice guidance relating to early special measures meetings:

- Such meetings should take place as soon as possible after the need for one has been identified (para 24). This effectively means that the meeting can take place either during the course of an investigation (eg prior to an interview) or after the submission of a case file to the CPS.

- The police are responsible for identifying those cases in which an early special measures meeting is appropriate during the course of an investigation (para 19) but the prosecutor may request an early special measures meeting where he/she considers it to be appropriate after having reviewed the case file (para 21).
- It is accepted that early special measures meetings will not always be necessary, eg where an application for special measures is a foregone conclusion because it relates to the use of video-recorded evidence-in-chief for a child witness in a sexual assault case (para 22).
- If necessary, early special measures meeting can take place over the telephone where the case is straightforward or urgent (para 39).
- A record should be made of the meetings and the agreements reached at it on a form set out in Annex A of the practice guidance (para 39). This can be done by means of exchanging facsimile messages where the meeting takes place over the telephone.

6.5 Chapter Summary

The special measures set out in the YJCEA are:

- Screens;
- Live TV link;
- Evidence in private;
- Removal of wigs and gowns;
- Video-recorded evidence-in-chief;
- Video-recorded cross-examination;
- Intermediaries; and
- Communication aids.

Police have a responsibility to explain these measures to vulnerable and intimidated witnesses and to solicit their views about them.

Where it might be necessary to apply for something that does not feature in the YJCEA that might help the witness to give their best evidence, consideration can be given to inviting the court to make use of its inherent common law powers.

SPACE FOR NOTES

SPACE FOR NOTES

7

Consent: Whose Decision is it anyway?

7.1 **Introduction**

There are two main occasions when investigators may need to seek or obtain the informed consent from either a vulnerable adult or child who is a victim or witness to a criminal offence. These occasions are consent for a medical examination or consent to conduct a video-recorded interview.

There are various issues involved with obtaining consent; these will largely depend on the prevailing circumstances and of the investigator's particular involvement with the vulnerable adult or child witness.

Informed consent is best described as a process that includes the presentation of all the available relevant information to the adult or child witness, and that the adult or child fully understands the implications of giving their consent and of allowing them the scope and opportunity to ask questions about this and to have them answered. It is recommended that this decision-making process should be fully documented.

Because the implications of obtaining and recording consent differ between vulnerable adults and child victims and witnesses this chapter has been divided into two sections, firstly dealing with vulnerable adults, and secondly to deal with the issues surrounding children who are witnesses or victims of criminal offences. The issues surrounding a vulnerable adult or child who is suspected of either committing or being involved in the commission of a criminal offence are covered in the provisions of Code C, paras 11:15–11:18 of the Police and Criminal Evidence Act 1984.

7.2 **Vulnerable Adults**

The issues surrounding consent and vulnerable adults can be a complex affair. It must never be assumed that just because an adult witness or victim has some form of physical or learning disability that they are not capable of consenting to matters themselves. Denying a vulnerable adult the opportunity to give consent themselves when they are able to do so merely on the basis that they have been deemed vulnerable is an abuse in itself. However there will be occasions when investigators will have some form of involvement with a vulnerable adult who is either a victim or witness and there will be a requirement for them to obtain consent in order to undertake either a medical examination or visually recorded statement. This chapter will explain some of the issues surrounding the matter of consent and of how they can be dealt with effectively and in accordance with the published guidance. ABE, para 3.60 states that all witnesses should be given the opportunity to have their interview taped and that they should freely consent to this procedure.

The Mental Health Act 1983: Code of Practice (published 1999) defines consent as:

The voluntary and continuing permission of the adult to agree to a course of action or inaction, based on an adequate knowledge of the purpose, nature, likely effects and risks of the proposed action/inaction, including the likelihood of its success and any alternatives to it. Permission given under any unfair or undue pressure is not 'consent'.

It is important for investigators to understand that the law protects some categories of vulnerable adult who do not have the ability (capacity) to consent. These occurrences generally relate to sexual matters and relationships. It is also important to remember that it is against the law for staff in residential care homes to have a sexual relationship with a patient who is detained under the Mental Health Act. When there is any doubt at all as to the adult witness's capacity to give their own informed consent to be interviewed or take part in a forensic medical examination then appropriate steps should be taken to secure consent in accordance with published guidance.

Under common law, an adult must give informed consent before either a medical examination or a medical treatment can be provided. In order to give informed consent, a person must have the capacity to do so.

7.2.1 Capacity

The accepted principle that underpins issues relating to medical practice and the current law in respect of matters relating to capacity is that vulnerable adults should be: 'enabled and encouraged to take for themselves those decisions which they are able to take' (Law Commission Report No 231 (1995), para 2.46).

Capacity, however, is a term that may mean different things to different people who are involved with a vulnerable adult, and the means of assessment will vary from one profession to another. It should always be assumed that the person has the capacity to consent unless proven otherwise. The Mental Capacity Act 2005 describes a person who is lacking mental capacity as follows:

If at the time s/he is unable by reason of mental disability to make a decision for himself (or herself) on the matter in question; or s/he is unable to communicate his (her) decision on that matter because s/he is unconscious or for any other reason, a person should be regarded as unable to make a decision because of mental disability if the disability is such that, at the time that the decision needs to be made, the person is unable to understand or retain the information relevant to the decision; or unable to make a decision based on that information (Making Decisions: Lord Chancellor's Department, 1999).

Sections 1 to 8 of Pt I of the Mental Capacity Act 2005 are reproduced in Appendix B for reference.

Best interests

Where it is thought that a vulnerable adult lacks capacity in relation to making a specific decision, then that decision must be made in that vulnerable adult's best interest. The only interests that should be considered and taken into account are those of the person in question. It will not be considered lawful to allow the views and ideas of social services, medical professionals, and police investigators to override what is clearly in the person's best interests simply to further an investigation.

In relation to deciding whether or not any medical treatment should be provided, or what form that intervention should take in relation to someone who lacks capacity, the House of Lords has defined best interest as medical treatment, which is:

> The voluntary and continuing permission of the adult to agree to a course of action or inaction, based on an adequate knowledge of the purpose, nature, likely effects and risks of the proposed action/inaction, including the likelihood of its success and any alternatives to it. Permission given under any unfair or undue pressure is not 'consent' (Code of Practice: Mental Health Act 1983).

Alternatively, in urgent cases, 'best interests' are defined with reference to medical treatment as that which is:

> Necessary to save life or prevent deterioration or ensure an improvement in the patient's physical or mental health; and in accordance with a practice accepted at the time by a responsible body of medical opinion skilled in the particular form of treatment in question (ibid).

In other aspects of decision-making the law is less clear. However, it is recommended that in when making any decision as to what is in the best interest of any vulnerable adult, consideration should be given to the following areas:

- The ascertainable past and present wishes and feelings of the vulnerable adult concerned and the factors the vulnerable adult would consider, if able to do so;
- The need to permit and encourage the person to participate or improve his or her ability to participate, as fully as possible, in anything done for, and any decision affecting, him or her;
- The views of other people whom it is appropriate and practical to consult about the person's wishes and feelings and what would be in his or her best interests, eg:
    (i) any person named by him or her as someone to be consulted on those matters;
    (ii) anyone engaged in caring for him or her or interested in his or her welfare;
    (iii) the holder of any enduring power of attorney granted by him or her;
    (iv) any manager appointed by the court.
- Whether the purpose for which any action or decision is required can be as effectively achieved in a manner less restrictive of the person's freedom of action.

Best interests meetings

No one person can give consent on behalf of a person who lacks the capacity to make decisions for themselves. It should rather be a meeting of all those concerned with the person and their best interests, whoever they may be, where all views are expressed freely and the pros and cons carefully weighed and balanced. If the person concerned had previously been involved in a situation similar to the one currently the subject of the meeting and on that occasion they had the capacity to give their own consent and they chose not to take part in the event in question, be that a visually recorded statement or medical examination, then this would have to given significant weight when making decisions now.

Human rights considerations

There are various matters that need to be taken into account when considering human rights issues. Investigators need to carefully balance the vulnerable adult's rights and needs as provided for them under the Human Rights Act against the need to conduct an effective investigation. The needs of an investigator and the rights of an individual may not always be compatible, therefore, the balancing act will need to be well considered and not made rashly, but with perhaps a more holistic view than would normally be taken. Below is a list of the human rights articles that will impact most on a vulnerable adult and the issues that surround consent.

Article 6

Everyone has the right to recognition everywhere as a person before the law.

Article 7

All are equal before the law and are entitled without any discrimination to equal protection of the law. All are entitled to equal protection against any discrimination in violation of this Declaration and against any incitement to such discrimination.

Article 8

Everyone has the right to an effective remedy by the competent national tribunals for acts violating the fundamental rights granted him by the constitution or by law.

Article 12

No one shall be subjected to arbitrary interference with his privacy, family, home or correspondence, nor to attacks upon his honour and reputation. Everyone has the right to the protection of the law against such interference or attacks.

7.3 **Children**

The issue of conducting medical examinations or obtaining medical treatment for children is one that has always been the subject of interpretation, it is hoped that this chapter will go some way to explaining the true position.

7.3.1 **Medical examinations**

The decision to conduct a medical examination of a child, whether it is a simple examination to tend to a superficial abrasion or a more intrusive forensic medical examination in a serious sexual assault case, will require a level of consent from someone. Who this is, will largely depend on the age of the child. In the case of young children this will nearly always be a parent or guardian who has parental responsibility for that child or young person.

The general medical council have strict guidelines about this issue that must be adhered to before a paediatrician or medical practitioner will begin to conduct any form of medical intervention. In certain circumstances the medical practitioner or paediatrician will accept the consent of the child or young person themselves depending on their age and whether that person is capable of understanding not only the procedure itself, but also the implications of that procedure. The decision as to whether the doctor accepts the child's own consent will rest entirely with the doctor.

The Family Law Reform Act 1969 gives competent young people between the ages of 16 and 18 the ability in law to consent to medical treatment. If there is conflict, however, the matter will need to be referred to the court.

Example—Medical examinations and consent

If the procedure is minor and only involves the cleaning of a superficial skin injury and the application of a plaster then the doctor may consider that a 14-year-old has sufficient understanding to give his or her own consent to this procedure. If, however, it is a more complicated injury that requires a more invasive approach, such as an operation, they may equally think that that the child or young person doesn't have the capacity to fully understand the full implications of such an intervention and associated risks involved in a general anaesthetic or the possible consequences of it. They may then require consent from a parent or guardian for that child.

7.3.2 **Video-recorded interviews**

The Home Office Guidance contained in *Achieving Best Evidence in Criminal Proceedings* (ABE) is clear about the issue of consent before a child or young person under 17 years of age can be interviewed. The interviewee must give their consent before the start of the interview.

The interview should only proceed after the full implications of the interview, including the issues surrounding any subsequent court appearance and giving evidence, have been fully explained and the interviewer is certain that the witness has fully understood them.

Consent in this context could almost be described as an implied concept, and is demonstrated by the witness sitting unrestrained and of their own free will in a chair talking to the interviewer, and in the majority of cases the child is brought to the interview suite by a parent or guardian who is happy to allow the interview to take place. The interview will nearly always be visually recorded (primary rule) and this will tend to demonstrate that the witness has not been coerced into making the statement (it will be immediately apparent to anyone watching if they have been).

POINT TO NOTE—CONSENT

ABE, para 2.68 states:

That on every occasion that consent is sought from a witness the interviewer should take all steps to inform the witness as to the purpose of the interview. This must be expl ained in a manner that is appropriate to the age and development of the witness.

In the case of young children the consent of a parent or guardian will be required, however there is no longer a requirement to obtain the written consent to interview a child from a parent or guardian in all cases, however it is essential to record the fact that consent has been sought, what the parent or guardian were told, and to who and when this information was given.

7.3.3 **Parental responsibility**

Mothers automatically gain parental responsibility for their child at birth; fathers only have parental responsibility if they were married to the mother of the child at the time of the child's birth. However, if the father was not married to the mother he can obtain parental responsibility by making a formal agreement with the mother or by obtaining a court order.

From 1 December 2003, fathers who register a child's birth with the mother automatically gain parental responsibility. This is not retrospective, and will therefore only apply to children who are registered after 1 December 2003. If the father's name was not on the birth certificate before 1 December 2003, he can apply with the mother's agreement to re-register the birth of the child and thereby gain parental responsibility.

If a child lives with a member of his or her family other than his or her parents (eg grandparents, aunt or uncle, or older brother or sister) or with someone else, those people may obtain parental responsibility for the child or an application can be made to the court for a Residence Order or Special Guardianship Order (adoption).

Parents have parental responsibility until a child reaches the age of 18 years. If the child is the subject of a care order, the local authority has parental responsibility until the child has attained the age of 18 years unless this order is discharged. Where people with Residence Orders also have parental responsibility, they have responsibility until the child is either 16 or 18, depending on when the order expires.

Particular caution will be required if a child or young person is described as being 'in care' under the terms of the Children Act 1989 which places a responsibility on agencies to work whenever possible in partnership with the parents of children with whom they are involved.

If a child has been made a ward of court then prior to any decision as to whether a visually recorded statement or medical examination takes place the court must on all occasions be consulted and give its authority for the requested intervention to take place. In practice, there are very few 'wards of court' and therefore this occurrence is likely to be rare.

Authority to conduct a video-recorded interview can be granted by the family court as a specific attachment to an order issued by the court. This will however have to be requested at the time of application for the order. If parents/carers refuse their consent, investigators should seek advice from their partner agencies or legal departments about how to proceed. This may entail an application being made to the Family Court for either:

- An Emergency Protection Order (s 44 of the Children Act 1989) in urgent situations;
- An Assessment Order (s 43 of the Children Act 1989) where full assessment is required;
- A Specific Issue Order (s 8 of the Children Act 1989) where issues relate to questioning parental responsibility.

7.3.4 Children's rights

The Convention on the Rights of the Child was adopted and opened for signature, ratification, and accession by General Assembly Resolution 44/25 of 20 November 1989.

The rights of children are protected in this international convention, to which the UK is a signatory; this declaration contains numerous articles that deal with the varying issues surrounding children and their treatment and welfare. Below is a list of some of the more pertinent articles contained in the Convention to which investigators should pay particular attention when considering the issues of consent. The Convention declares:

Article 1

For the purposes of the present Convention, a child means every human being below the age of eighteen years unless under the law applicable to the child, majority is attained earlier.

Article 3(1)

In all actions concerning children, whether undertaken by public or private social welfare institutions, courts of law, administrative authorities or legislative bodies, the best interests of the child shall be a primary consideration.

Article 12(1) and (2)

Parties shall assure to the child who is capable of forming his or her own views the right to express those views freely in all matters affecting the child, the views of the child being given due weight in accordance with the age and maturity of the child.

For this purpose, the child shall in particular be provided the opportunity to be heard in any judicial and administrative proceedings affecting the child, either directly, or through a representative or an appropriate body, in a manner consistent with the procedural rules of national law.

Article 13(1) and (2)

The child shall have the right to freedom of expression; this right shall include freedom to seek, receive and impart information and ideas of all kinds, regardless of frontiers, either orally, in writing or in print, in the form of art, or through any other media of the child's choice.

The exercise of this right may be subject to certain restrictions, but these shall only be such as are provided by law and are necessary:

(a) For respect of the rights or reputations of others; or
(b) For the protection of national security or of public order, or of public health or morals.

Article 16(1) and (2)

No child shall be subjected to arbitrary or unlawful interference with his or her privacy, family, home or correspondence, nor to unlawful attacks on his or her honour and reputation.

The child has the right to the protection of the law against such interference or attacks.

Article 18(1)

Parties shall use their best efforts to ensure recognition of the principle that both parents have common responsibilities for the upbringing and development of the child. Parents or, as the case may be, legal guardians, have the primary responsibility for the upbringing and development of the child. The best interests of the child will be their basic concern.

Article 19(1) and (2)

Parties shall take all appropriate legislative, administrative, social and educational measures to protect the child from all forms of physical or mental violence, injury or abuse, neglect or negligent treatment, maltreatment or exploitation, including sexual abuse, while in the care of parent(s), legal guardian(s) or any other person who has the care of the child.

Such protective measures should, as appropriate, include effective procedures for the establishment of social programmes to provide necessary support for the child and for those who have the care of the child, as well as for other forms of prevention and for identification, reporting, referral, investigation, treatment and follow-up of instances of child maltreatment described heretofore, and, as appropriate, for judicial involvement.

These rights have an implication for professionals who interact with children and young people within the context of a criminal investigation, as the rights enshrined in the declaration may not always reflect what is perceived by professionals to always be in the best interests of a criminal investigation or those of the child themselves.

Example—Mental capacity and 'best interests'

If an interviewer seeks consent from a 14-year-old child to be interviewed about an incident of stranger abuse, and after fully explaining the procedures and implications of such an interview to the child, they give their consent, which is subsequently supported by their parent or guardian, and this process is fully documented, there is unlikely to be a problem with the issue of consent later.

DISCUSSION POINT

Refusal of parental consent for visually recorded interview

If a 14-year-old child who is the victim of a criminal offence wants to take part in a visually recorded interview and tell the police exactly what has happened to them, and the child's parents who are not suspected of being involved in the alleged abuse firmly state that they do not wish their child to be party to any such interview as they know how harrowing a criminal court case can be for a young witness, and that it is not in the child's best interest to be interviewed, what would you do?

7.4 Human Rights Considerations

As with the Convention on the Rights of the Child, there are also various matters that need to be considered under the heading of human rights issues. As with the previous section on children's rights, it is important to carefully balance the child's rights as provided under the Human Rights Act and the Convention of the Rights of the Child and their participation in a criminal investigation as a victim or witness, when keeping in mind the 'Best interests of the child'. There are three main articles under the Human Rights Act that may impact on the way we deal with children within a criminal justice setting.

Article 6

Everyone has the right to recognition everywhere as a person before the law.

Article 7

All are equal before the law and are entitled without any discrimination to equal protection of the law. All are entitled to equal protection against any discrimination in violation of this Declaration and against any incitement to such discrimination.

Article 8

Everyone has the right to an effective remedy by the competent national tribunals for acts violating the fundamental rights granted him by the constitution or by law.

7.4.1 Fraser competency

It was not until 1985 that the position concerning younger children was considered by the House of Lords in the case of *Gillick v West Norfolk and Wisbech Area Health Authority* [1985] 3 All ER 403. The Gillick, or Fraser principle as it is now known, arises out of a civil court case, and concerns the rights of parents in relation to medical matters concerning their children.

The case concerned a teenage child's right to consent to medical treatment without the parents' knowledge. The 14-year-old child went to see the family GP and asked to be prescribed the birth control pill. The GP agreed to this request and respected the request from the child not to tell her parents about this. The mother (Victoria Gillick) later found out about this and took the Health Authority to court stating that she should have been informed about this request prior to the prescription being written and have been asked for her consent.

The court did not recognize any rule of absolute parental authority until a fixed age. Instead, parental rights were recognized by the law only as long as they were needed for the protection of the child and such rights yielded to the child's right to make their own decisions when they reached a sufficient understanding and intelligence to be capable of making up their own mind.

Thus regarding parental involvement in the decision-making process in matters about a child or young person's life, Lord Fraser said that the degree of parental control varied according to the child's understanding and intelligence.

During the ruling Lord Scarman opined that parental rights only existed so long as they were needed to protect the property and person of the child. He said:

> As a matter of law the parental right to determine whether or not their minor child below the age of 16 will have medical treatment terminates if and when the child achieves sufficient understanding and intelligence to enable him to understand fully what is proposed.

It therefore follows that the older a child or young person becomes the less reliant they are on their parent or guardian and the more able they are to make life changing decisions for themselves. This case, however, carries no weight in the Criminal Court, and can only be used as a rule of thumb. Subsequent changes have led to this matter being renamed after the judge rather than the plaintiff Mrs Gillick; it is now referred to as the Fraser principle.

Subsequent attempts by medical professionals to further clarify the law were specifically discouraged by the courts. It became a matter for the doctor to judge whether a child under 16 was 'Gillick competent'. The result is that a doctor, if he or she judges the child to be 'Gillick competent', can only disclose information to the parent with the child's consent, regardless of parental responsibility.

POINT TO NOTE—PARENTAL RIGHTS

Parental rights to control a child do not exist for the benefit of the parent. They exist for the benefit of the child and they are justified only insofar as they enable the parent to perform his duties towards the child and towards other children in the family.

Lord Fraser of Telly Belton

7.5 Chapter Summary

This chapter has explored the complex issue of consent. To this end, it has examined the issues that relate to the consent of children and of vulnerable adults in investigative contexts relating to interviews and medical examinations.

SPACE FOR NOTES

SPACE FOR NOTES

8

Competence and Compellability

8.1 **Introduction**

When investigators talk about competence and compellability, what they are really talking about is effectively a two-stage test:

(1) Is the witness capable of giving evidence?
(2) Can the witness be forced (compelled) to give evidence?

Whether or not a witness is to be considered competent (capable) to make a statement and then go on to give evidence in a criminal trial is one of the first hurdles that investigators will have to jump when making decisions about witnesses.

The judiciary has long debated the issues relating to the competence of child witnesses, both in and out of court, but the arguments relating to adult witnesses have to a large extent still to be had. This is because in the main interviewers have not taken statements from adult witnesses when competence may become an issue for them at court.

Once investigators have decided whether the witness is capable of giving a statement, they need to decide whether they can then be compelled (forced) to give evidence. In the main, any witness (other than the defendant and the spouse of the defendant in certain circumstances) is theoretically compellable, however, persons with diplomatic immunity are not compellable in any proceedings.

8.2 **Compellability**

There are no special rules governing the issue of compellability of vulnerable adults and child witnesses in criminal proceedings although, of course, there are rules concerning the competence of such witnesses, and it is accepted that a witness who is not competent can never be deemed to be compellable.

The matter of whether a partner (spouse) is compellable or not is a complex issue. The rules relating to compellability of partners (spouses) will apply also to same-sex couples in a registered civil partnership.

These limitations on compellability apply only to people who are actually married at the time of the hearing. However, once a witness has taken the oath, and has given evidence, the fact that the witness was not compellable is irrelevant.

Explanation of Compellability

At present, the rules in respect of compellability in criminal cases are defined in s 80 of the Police and Criminal Evidence Act 1984.

If X and Y are married (or civil partners):

- Y is compellable for the defence of X (s 80(2)), unless Y is a co-defendant with X in the same proceedings (s 80(4));

- Y is compellable for the defence of any co-defendant of X (s 80(2A)) only if the offence committed by that co-defendant is one of the 'specified offences' in s 80(3), and so long as Y is not a co-defendant in the same proceedings.
- Y is compellable for the prosecution of X, or any co-defendant of X, if the offence is one of the specified offences in s 80(3). The question whether Y is compellable if he or she is a co-defendant does not arise, because no defendant is *competent* for the prosecution.

As can be seen, the issue of compellability of a spouse is most tortuous where the spouse is also a defendant in the same proceedings. If that is the case, he or she cannot be compelled to give evidence if to do so would mean that he or she was giving evidence for his or her own prosecution. However, once Y ceases to be a co-defendant, this protection is lost. Y then becomes compellable for the defence of X, and for the defence or prosecution of X if the charge is one of the 'specified offences'. The most usual way in which Y ceases to be a co-defendant is for him to plead guilty. However, if the prosecution discontinues the case against Y, this will have the same effect.

POINT TO NOTE—COMPELLABILITY OF THE SPOUSE OF AN ACCUSED PERSON

The 'specified offences' in s 80(3) of the Police and Criminal Evidence Act are:

- those that involve injury or threat of injury to the spouse or civil partner or a person under 16 years of age;
- any sexual offence against a person under 16 years of age;
- attempting or conspiring to commit any of the above, or inciting anyone else to do so.

In summary,
A person is not compellable against his or her spouse or civil partner except where the offence is against the spouse or civil partner and it involves violence, or it is a sexual or violent offence against a child.

   A person is compellable on behalf of his or her spouse or civil partner unless that would have the effect of a defendant being called by the prosecution.

   The fact that a person's spouse or civil partner refuses to give evidence in proceedings against that person may be prejudicial to the defendant. After all, if the spouse or civil partner clearly has information relevant to the case, but refuses to expose it in court, it can look as if something is being concealed. Of course, there are likely to be good reasons why a person does not wish to give evidence in the prosecution of his or her spouse or civil partner, and by s 80A, the prosecution may not comment on their failure to give evidence.

   There have often been calls for changes in the law in this area, because in some child abuse cases it is not clear which of the parents is the culprit and, if both are charged, neither can be compelled to give evidence.

An 'Acaster warning' (*R v Acaster* (1912) 7 Cr App R 187) is a warning to a person who is about to give evidence against his/her spouse that he/she cannot be compelled to do so. In addition to this, in *R v Pitt* [1983] QB 25 the Court of Appeal said that it was desirable that any wife be warned that she is not obliged to give evidence against her husband before she takes the oath. Presumably this direction would apply to men giving evidence against their wives, too.

The rules are, however, somewhat different in civil proceedings because the Evidence Act 1851 and the Evidence Amendment Act 1853 point out that any competent witness is compellable for any party in a civil hearing. This includes the parties to the hearing, their spouses, and any child or vulnerable adult who is judged competent.

8.3 **Competence**

There has never been an issue about the competence of adult witnesses, their evidence has in the past having been presented in a written format and served accordingly. It is only now that investigators have become more inclusive in the way that they gather evidence that the issues of competence have needed to be taken into consideration.

The general principle relating to competence is set out in s 53(1) of the Youth Justice and Criminal Evidence Act 1999 and states that at every stage in criminal proceedings all persons (whatever their age may be) will be considered to be competent to give evidence in criminal proceedings. However, it is the responsibility of the person or organization who wishes to call the person as a witness to satisfy the court that the witness is competent. When making such decisions, the use of special measures to assist the witness and protect them while they are giving their evidence must be taken into consideration.

Scenario—Competence

In this judgment, the court of appeal rejected a submission by the defence that it was not in the interests of justice to admit the video-recorded evidence-in-chief of a sexual assault victim with Alzheimer's disease on the basis of her competence.

R v D (2002) *RVD* [2002] 3 WLR 997

The defence appealed against a decision to admit the video recorded evidence of an 81-year-old woman suffering from Alzheimer's disease, who the defendant was accused of raping. Disallowing the appeal, the Court of Appeal held that the video-recorded evidence was admissible in the interests of justice under s 26 of the Criminal Justice Act, and further, that there was no bar to its admission under Article 6 of the European Convention on Human Rights (right to a fair trial). This judgment was further upheld in a similar appeal case involving Alzheimer's disease in *R v Sed* [2004] EWCA Crim 1294.

Scenario—Sworn testimony

In this judgment, the Court of Appeal rejected a submission by the defence that children aged 11 and 12 were too young to give sworn evidence.

R v Hayes (1976)

The defendant was convicted after the trial judge allowed children aged 11 and 12 to give sworn evidence. On appeal the defendant contended that these children were too young to appreciate the nature of the oath, and their evidence should not have been admitted. However, the Court of Appeal held that the important factors in determining whether a witness should be sworn were whether the witness appreciated the solemnity of the occasion, and understood the importance of telling the truth. Consequently the appeal was dismissed.

In relation to child witnesses, it has also been deemed that all witnesses in order to be considered competent must be able to understand questions that are put to them and be able to give intelligible answers.

Therefore, as long as a witness who is over 14 years of age passes the test as shown above, there is no reason why they will not be able to give sworn testimony. However, investigators will need to remember that a child over 14 can only give sworn evidence if he or she has a 'sufficient appreciation of the solemnity of the occasion and of the particular responsibility to tell the truth'. It is an accepted principle, however, that a child who is under 14 years of age cannot give sworn testimony,

8.4 **Chapter Summary**

It is important to note that there may be occasions when a witness may be deemed as not being compellable. These occasions are likely to be rare, however, and will probably be as a result of the witness having diplomatic immunity and therefore not be compellable in criminal proceedings.

The issue of competence is quite simple, as long as the vulnerable adult or child witness is capable of understanding questions that are put to them and is able to respond in a way that can be understood by the court with the assistance of 'special measures' then they will be considered to be competent.

SPACE FOR NOTES

SPACE FOR NOTES

SPACE FOR NOTES

9

Medical Examinations

9.1 **Introduction**

This section describes the doctor's role in an examination or assessment of a child or vulnerable adult for protection purposes; what to do if the person refuses examination or assessment, and the role of the expert witness.

The touching of patients without valid consent is potentially battery. The legal position with regard to children is complex. If the patient is competent and gives consent then such consent is normally valid. The broad position therefore in English law with regard to the examination of vulnerable adult patients, or patients who are under the age of 18 years, is that such examination would not constitute battery if valid consent for the examination has been given either by a person or persons with the appropriate authority, a person who has parental responsibility, or by the vulnerable adult or child, if they are competent to give their own consent.

Throughout this chapter please read 'persons' for 'vulnerable adults or children'.

9.2 **Why Is a Medical Examination Necessary?**

When a vulnerable adult or child has been the subject of abuse, or a statutory agency suspect or is concerned that a vulnerable adult or child may have been subjected to abuse, a medical examination of that person may be required for several reasons:

- To ascertain whether a vulnerable adult or child is in need of immediate medical attention or has experienced physical harm that may require medical intervention and treatment;
- To ascertain whether there is evidence of physical, sexual, emotional harm, or neglect that would support an allegation of abuse;
- To harvest forensic samples when appropriate.

9.3 **When Should a Person Be Medically Examined?**

With the exception of situations in which the health of the vulnerable adult, child, or young person is a cause for concern, the medical examination should normally be undertaken after the child and family have been seen by the police. This examination or treatment should be carried out at a time that is not likely to further disrupt the person's normal routine, unless the requirement for such intervention is urgent.

Any medical examination should not be used as a means to determine whether an offence has been committed or if a multi-agency investigation is required because, in the absence of a police investigation, it may be unclear whether any medical examination is in fact appropriate or even required. The effect of this is that the person may be subjected to an unwarranted and completely unnecessary intimate examination. The police investigation should inform the medical assessment, ensuring that the correct type of medical intervention is undertaken. This should reduce the risk of repeated examinations.

9.4 **Where Should a Medical Examination Take Place?**

Any medical examination should be undertaken in a calm and sensitive manner and in the case of children, with appropriate decoration and play materials in order to reduce the stress and anxiety of the child and his/her family. It is also extremely important that any staff who are present are familiar with the needs of the person and experienced in working with people in distressing situations.

It may occasionally be necessary to undertake a medical examination in a hospital accident and emergency unit, or forensic suite. These occasions should be rare, and medical practitioners and staff should be aware that these venues may be particularly distressing and may in fact make a distressing situation even worse.

9.5 **Where and by Whom Should a Person Be Seen?**

When a person appears to have urgent medical needs and is unwell, their condition must be addressed as a matter of urgency at the most appropriate location, and by staff who have the most suitable facilities to cope with the situation most appropriately, for example an Accident and Emergency Unit or a paediatric ward in a hospital.

Where a child been presented at hospital by a parent or carer and it is clear that they have sustained injuries for which there is no adequate explanation or where the injuries are inconsistent with the explanation given by the carer or parent, the police and social services should be informed without any undue delay, and an assessment by a consultant community paediatrician should be requested.

Where a person has disclosed that they have been subjected to any form of sexual abuse, consideration should be given to the person being given a forensic examination when samples can be harvested in the most appropriate and forensically safe way. However, a strategy meeting or discussion should take place before any decisions are reached. This will prevent an unnecessary forensic examination with a vulnerable adult or child in the event that no penetration of a body orifice has taken place.

The purpose of any joint medical examination is to reduce the number of practitioners and number of occasions on which a person will need to be seen. On occasions and depending on the reason for the medical intervention it may be appropriate that the examination takes place with a member of the GUM team to assess the risk of sexually transmitted disease.

> **POINT TO NOTE—EXAMINATIONS**
>
> All examinations should wherever possible be undertaken by two practitioners who, at a minimum, have the core skills laid out in the Guidance for Paediatric Forensic Examinations in relation to possible Child Sexual Abuse.
>
> Royal College of Paediatrics and Child Health Association of Forensic Physicians, September 2004

9.6 The Need for Consent

Except in an emergency, any examination or assessment which involves physical contact with any person requires consent (from a competent child, a parent, a carer, or another person with parental responsibility), or with authority from a court. Even if required assessment does not involve any physical contact, for example an interview as part of a psychological or psychiatric assessment, consent from the person is still required. In exceptional circumstances, particularly with vulnerable adults or young children, it may be in the best interests of that person to undergo an examination without explicit consent. These circumstances would require clear justification based upon an informed judgment of the best interests of the person concerned. In these circumstances doctors should make a clear record of the decision to go ahead, and its justification in the person's medical notes. In the case of medical examinations on children, the courts have emphasized that it is harmful for children to be exposed to an unnecessarily large number of assessments.

In the case of *Re CS*, the High Court heard that a child had been subjected to 12 intimate physical examinations by the same doctor. Bracewell J said:

> By reason of the failure of the court to control the examination of [the child], she was, in my judgment, subjected to abusive intimate examinations on more occasions than could possibly be justified.

9.7 The Legal Situation in Relation to Children

In relation to children, once any legal proceedings have started, the court becomes responsible for making the decision as to whether any type of assessment is required for the purposes of the civil proceedings, while having regard to the child's welfare. However, there is a danger that children may be repeatedly assessed before the court proceedings have been initiated.

Example—Concerns about unnecessary child assessments

If the parents are separated and one parent is convinced that the other parent is abusive, they may seek medical evidence to confirm this. In other cases, a parent may agree to a series of assessments at the request of the social services, only because they are worried that if they do not co-operate with the social services, the local authority will initiate care proceedings against them and remove their child.

In such situations, where it is apparent that there are concerns that unnecessary medical examinations or assessments are being carried out, consideration should be given to obtaining a court order, prohibiting a parent from granting consent for any further examinations or assessments.

Where a child is the subject of police protection, the police do not have parental responsibility. The consent of a parent and the child must be obtained.

Where a child is the subject of a child assessment order, the court can give directions regarding and medical examinations or assessments.

If the child is the subject of an Emergency Protection Order, the local authority is granted limited parental responsibility. The court can give social services the authority to obtain a medical, psychiatric examination, or conduct an investigative interview with a child.

Once family proceedings under the Children Act (or its equivalent in other UK jurisdictions) have been initiated, the court is responsible for making any decisions that may affect the conduct of the proceedings, including whether any medical examinations or assessments are appropriate.

POINT TO NOTE—EXAMINATION OR ASSESSMENTS OF CHILDREN

The Family Proceedings Rules 1991 state:

No person may, without the leave of the court, cause the child to be medically or psychiatrically examined, or otherwise assessed, for the purpose of the preparation of expert evidence for use in the proceedings.

Therefore, in civil proceedings, before undertaking any medical examination or assessment for the purpose of proceedings, any medical professionals should confirm that the court has granted permission (known as 'leave') for the assessment before undertaking any such assessments.

Obviously this requirement does not prevent any assessment which is necessary for the child's health. In addition, when the court makes certain orders, it can positively direct that an assessment should take place, or that no medical examination of the child takes place.

POINT TO NOTE—DIRECTION OF THE COURT REGARDING EXAMINATIONS OR ASSESSMENTS

The Children Act 1989, s 38(6) and (7) states:

Where the court makes an interim care order, or interim supervision order, it may give such directions (if any) as it considers appropriate with regard to the medical or psychiatric examination or other assessment of the child; but if the child is of sufficient understanding to make an informed decision he may refuse to submit to the examination or other assessment.

[Such] a direction [. . .] may be to the effect that there is to be:

(a) No such examination or assessment; or

(b) No such examination or assessment unless the court directs otherwise.

It is important to note that the sections of the Children Act which allow the court to direct that a medical examination or assessment should take place also state that a child who is of 'sufficient understanding to make an informed decision' may refuse to be the subject of any medical examination or assessment.

Therefore, even when the court directs that a medical examination or assessment takes place, a professional will still need to obtain the consent from that person if they are considered to be competent to make such a decision.

9.7.1 Lack of co-operation by the child

Where a child refuses to co-operate with an assessment, there are several possibilities.

It may be decided that assessment is impossible without the child's co-operation: in this case legal advice should be sought.

An authorized assessment can lawfully proceed despite the child's objections, although health professionals may well be unwilling to proceed in these circumstances. If it is likely to be necessary to use force or sedatives to overcome the child's resistance, legal advice should be sought.

The court has no power under the Children Act to override the child's refusal to take part in a medical examination or assessment. However, in the case of *South Glamorgan County Council v W and B* [1993] 1 FLR 574, it was decided that the High Court exercising its 'inherent jurisdiction' may authorize an assessment against the wishes of a competent child if the child would otherwise be likely to suffer 'significant harm'. This decision was made in the High Court and is, therefore, not applicable to Magistrates' or county courts. Conducting a medical examination or assessment on a reluctant child is clearly controversial. Any such examination or assessment is unlikely to be appropriate unless the following apply:

- There is a high probability that useful evidence can be obtained;
- The evidence cannot be obtained in any other way; and
- The benefit to the child from obtaining the evidence outweighs the burdens involved in imposing the assessment on the child.

9.8 **Chapter Summary**

Doctors are, and are likely to remain, central to the provision of good care and support for vulnerable children and their families. The Victoria Climbié Inquiry Report (HMSO, 2003) drew attention both to the tragedy of child abuse, and to the complex, multi-agency response that is required to combat it. Where several different agencies or professionals share joint responsibility, however, it is clearly possible for vulnerable children to be overlooked. Where doctors have concerns about a child who may be at risk of abuse or neglect, it is essential that these concerns are acted upon, in accordance with the guidance in this note, or other local and national protocols. Where suspicions of abuse or neglect have been raised, doctors must ensure that their concerns, and the actions they have either taken, or intend to take, including any discussion with colleagues or professionals in other agencies are clearly recorded in the child or children's medical record. Where doctors have raised concerns about a child with colleagues or with other agencies and no action is regarded as necessary, doctors must ensure that all individual concerns have been properly recognised and responded to.

When working with children who may be at risk of neglect or abuse, doctors should judge each case on its merits, taking into consideration the likely degree of risk to the child or children involved. Disclosure of information between professionals from different agencies should always take place within an established system and be subject to a recognized protocol. This guidance applies equally to information about children who may be subject to abuse as well as to information about third parties, such as adults who may pose a threat to a child.

There is, finally, a need for both further evidence based research and medical education and training in this field. Professionals working in this area should therefore try actively to encourage and promote these activities.

SPACE FOR NOTES

SPACE FOR NOTES

SPACE FOR NOTES

10

Witness Interview
Strategies

10.1 **Introduction**

There can often be a great deal of confusion about the difference between an interview strategy and an interview plan to the extent that the terms are often used interchangeably. For the sake of clarity, this chapter considers a strategy to be a high-level overview of the interview in the context of the overall investigation, whereas a plan focuses on the tactical considerations applicable to the interview itself and on the preparation of a witness for an interview. While strategies and plans are mutually dependent on each other, they are separate entities in their own right. Responsibility for the strategy falls to the investigator, or somebody that the investigator has delegated with this responsibility where the case is complex (for example, an interview adviser). Responsibility for the plan falls to the interviewer. In some instances, it will be the case that the investigator and the interviewer are the same person.

The focus of this chapter is on witness interview strategies and their relationship to witness interview plans. Witness interview plans are considered in more detail in the chapters that follow.

10.2 **Components of a Witness Interview Strategy**

A witness interview strategy consists of 19 stages. While these stages are in principle sequential, in practice there can be some overlap between them.

10.2.1 **Stage 1: Review any relevant existing material that is available**

Prior to embarking on a witness interview strategy, all the relevant material already gathered by the investigation should be reviewed. While in some cases this might be fairly minimal, in others it could include:

- Material relating to any previous contact between the witness and agencies such as the police and social care services;
- Records of any initial complaint made by the witness;
- Records made by the first police officer or social worker on the scene of an alleged offence;
- Records made by any family liaison officer or victim liaison officer that relate to the witness;
- Records of any medical examination of the witness conducted in pursuit of the investigation;
- Video-recorded interviews already conducted with the witness or with other witnesses during the course of the investigation;
- Written statements already made by the witness or other witnesses during the course of the investigation;
- Records of any interview already conducted with or unsolicited comments made by an alleged offender.

10.2.2 **Stage 2: Debrief significant others involved in the investigation**

In this stage, consideration should be given to debriefing:

- The first police officer or social worker on the scene of an alleged offence;
- The first police officer or social worker to be told of the alleged offence by the witness;
- Any family liaison officer or victim liaison officer with information relating to the witness or the alleged offence;
- Interviewers who have already conducted interviews with other witnesses.

10.2.3 **Stage 3: Identify investigatively important information**

Investigatively important information falls into two categories: general investigative practice and case specific material.

Investigatively important information relating to general investigative practice includes:

- Points to prove any alleged offence(s);
- Information that should be considered when assessing a witness's identification evidence, as suggested in *R v Turnbull and Camelo* [1976] 63 Cr App R 132 and embodied in the mnemonic *ADVOKATE (Practical Guide to Investigative Interviewing*, published by Centrex, 2004):

  A Amount of time under observation

  D Distance from the eyewitness to the person/ incident

  V Visibility including time of day, street lighting, etc

  O Obstructions; anything getting in the way of the witness's view

  K Known or seen before; did the witness know, or had he or she seen the alleged perpetrator before?

  A Any reason to remember; was there something specific that made the person/incident memorable?

  T Time lapse; how long since the witness last saw the alleged perpetrator?

  E Errors or material discrepancies

- Any other people present at the time of the alleged offence;
- Anything said by the witness to a third party after the incident (evidence of first complaint, etc).

Investigatively important information amounting to case specific material includes:

- Where any items used in the commission of the alleged offence were disposed of (if the witness might have knowledge of this);
- Significant evidential inconsistencies between anything said by the witness and other material gathered during the investigation;

- Significant evidential omissions from any account given by the witness in respect of other material gathered during the investigation;
- Where the witness has knowledge of an alleged victim or a suspected perpetrator, an exploration of their relationship, background history, places frequented and any events related or similar to the alleged offence;
- Any background information that might enhance or detract from the credibility of the witness's account (eg the amount of any alcohol consumed, the nature of any drugs taken);
- Any information that the witness might have about the likelihood of witness intimidation (this should be dealt with after the witness's account has been covered to avoid confusion).

10.2.4 Stage 4: Consider the impact of other investigative strategies on the interview

Consideration should be given to the potential impact of the other aspects of the investigation on the interview. These other aspects of the investigation could include the:

- Forensic strategy;
- Identification strategy;
- Media strategy;
- Arrest strategy.

10.2.5 Stage 5: Identify sources of advice

Where the witness might be vulnerable, advice should be sought as to the best way to conduct the interview. Sources of advice will invariably include people who know the witness well (eg carers) and may include people who have expertise in respect of the witness's condition (eg health professionals). In either event, it is important to remember that these sources will not usually be conversant with the constraints of the criminal justice system. For this reason, the advice from these sources will need to be 'filtered' so that it takes account of the guidance set out in *Achieving Best Evidence* (ABE).

10.2.6 Stage 6: Assess the witness

The following issues should be taken into account when conducting a witness assessment:

- Which category or categories the witness falls into (ie vulnerable, intimidated, or significant);
- Any issues that will have an impact on the witness's consent;
- The extent to which the witness is likely to be co-operative/reluctant;

- What the witness is likely to have seen or heard, or otherwise experienced (based on what the witness has already said and what is known about the circumstances of the alleged offence).

10.2.7 Stage 7: Prioritize witness interviews

Where there is more than one witness to the alleged offence, some consideration will need to be given to the order in which the interviews are to take place. This should take account of:

- The probable significance of the witness's account (based on an assessment of what the witness is likely to have seen or heard, or otherwise experienced);
- Any apparent reluctance on the part of the witness that is likely to delay the interview;
- Any practical considerations impacting on access to the witness (eg as a result of a medical/psychological condition).

10.2.8 Stage 8: Set objectives for the interview

For the sake of clarity, the objectives set for the interview should be specific topic based (eg 'to obtain an account of what the witness saw, heard or otherwise experienced in the Dog and Duck public house on Saturday the 25th', 'to establish the nature of the witness's relationship with the alleged offender').

10.2.9 Stage 9: Consider the need for and practicality of an 'early special measures meeting' with the Crown Prosecution Service

An early special measures meeting can take place either before the interview or pre-trial, after the interview, or both (*Early Special Measures Meetings between the Police and the Crown Prosecution Service and Meetings between the Crown Prosecution Service and Vulnerable or Intimidated Witnesses*, Home Office, 2001). Police investigators are responsible for calling an early special measures meeting during the investigation, where this is necessary. These meetings are, in practice, usually telephone discussions the decisions of which are recorded on the form in Annex A of the document referred to above. The CPS can call an early special measures meeting if they consider it necessary after reviewing a case file sent to them by the police.

A pre-interview early special measures meeting should be considered in all cases other than where the only decision to be made is whether to video the interview or not and the decision to video-record the interview is a foregone conclusion (eg there is little point in calling a pre-interview early special measures meeting solely for the purposes of deciding whether to video the interview or not in circumstances where the primary rule applies (child witnesses in sexual or violent cases), unless there are the kind of 'insurmountable difficulties' to video recording that are mentioned in Vol 1 of ABE). Unless it is impractical to do so, a pre-interview early special measures meeting should take place where there is any doubt as to whether to video record the interview, where an intermediary or aids to communication are involved, or where there might be an issue about a supporter during the interview.

10.2.10 Stage 10: Identify resources

The following resources should be identified:

- Personnel;
  - Interviewer
  - Interview monitor
  - Reserve interviewer
  - Equipment operator
  - Intermediary
  - Interpreter
  - Interview supporter;
- Equipment and facilities;
  - Interview suite;
  - Video-recording equipment (number of cameras/microphones, DVD drives/ VHS recorders, screens where portable equipment is to be used);
  - Aids to communication (if required).

10.2.11 Stage 11: Consider the timing and location for the interview

Interviews need to take account of the witness's normal routine and the effects of any medication that they are taking. The impact of fatigue on the witness's ability to participate in the interview should be carefully considered; interviews should only be conducted with witnesses at times when they would usually be asleep in urgent circumstances and even then should only set out to obtain such information as is immediately necessary in the circumstances (a further interview may take place at a later time when the witness is refreshed). The impact of meal times should be similarly taken into account. The effects of any medication taken by the witness should also be considered; it should be remembered that some medication has a slow release effect so that a witness who, for example, takes a dose in the morning may not be drowsy until the afternoon.

The time spent travelling to and from an interview suite should be taken into consideration. Where necessary, this may need to be balanced against:

- Any forensic considerations in terms of possible cross-contamination arising from other witnesses using the suite;
- Any potential witness intimidation issues that might arise as a result of a witness using a suite in a place near to their home address;

- The kind of equipment available in the suite (some interviews, for example, those making use of sign language or symbol systems, may require more than the standard equipment of one pan tilt zoom and one wide-angle lens camera to effectively record the interaction taking place).

In some circumstances, it may be appropriate to conduct an interview in a place that is not a purpose built witness interview suite, for example, a witness's home address or a hospital. In these circumstances:

- Any portable equipment that is to be used should be capable of producing a recording of good sound and picture quality;
- The potential for background noise should be minimized as far as possible (the sound electrical devices elsewhere in the premises, such as radios and televisions, or sounds coming from outside the premises, such as children playing games or people repairing their vehicles, often appear louder when the recording is played back);
- The potential for visual clues about the location (particularly where the location is the witness's home address) or visual distractions in the background of the recording should be minimized as far as possible (the use of screens should be considered).

10.2.12 Stage 12: Consider what the interviewers are to be told about the offence and case specific investigatively important information in the initial briefing

While interviewers should know as much as possible about the witness, ideally they should know only a little about the alleged offence(s) before the interview. This is so because of the possibility that a detailed knowledge of the alleged offence might contaminate the interview process. Contamination might occur as a result of the interviewer:

(a) Inadvertently introducing information that has not already been mentioned by the witness in the interview; and

(b) Not asking all the questions that might otherwise have been asked due to any gaps or a lack of precision in the witness's account being sub-consciously supplemented with prior information about the offence.

However, in order to plan and prepare for the interview, interviewers will need a general knowledge of:

- The type of alleged offence(s);
- The approximate time and location of the alleged offence(s);
- A general knowledge of the scene of the alleged offence(s);
- How alleged offence came to the notice of police; and
- The nature of any intimidation.

While a limited knowledge of the alleged offence should be an aspiration, ABE acknowledges that circumstances and practical resource considerations might be such that the interviewers will know more about what is alleged than is ideal. These circumstances are particularly likely to arise where the interviewer is also involved extensively in the wider investigation, and where multiple witnesses are to be interviewed and only a limited number of interviewers are available. In these circumstances, interviewers should be mindful of the potential for such knowledge to contaminate the interview process in a bid to minimize its impact.

Given that ideally interviewers will only know a little about the offence, they should know only little if anything at all about investigatively important information amounting to case specific material prior to the interview. Where this material is not mentioned by the witness in their account amounts to a significant evidential omission, or results in a significant evidential inconsistency, it should be managed as set out in Chapter 11.

For the purpose of planning the interview, interviewers should, however, have an understanding of the kind of investigatively important information relating to general investigative practice that is likely to be relevant to the offence under investigation (case specific material and general investigative practice are more fully discussed at point 10.2.3 above).

10.2.13 Stage 13: Brief the interviewers and others involved in the interview process (eg intermediary, interpreter)

The person/people responsible for the interview strategy should tell interviewers about their role as soon as possible in order to give them the opportunity to fully plan and prepare for the interview. A briefing should be provided as a prelude to planning. This briefing should include:

- The category the witness falls into (ie vulnerable, intimidated, or significant);
- The objectives of the interview;
- The nature of the allegation;
- How the alleged offence came to the notice of police;
- Investigatively important information relating to general investigative practice to be included in the interview;
- Anything known about the witness including:
  - Previous involvement with the police or social services;
  - Whether an interpreter, intermediary, or aids to communication are required;
- Location for the interview and any recording equipment that is needed; and
- Means of contacting the investigation team (police and social services) in the event of any urgent actions arising from the interview.

Interviewers should have easy access to the investigation team when they are planning and preparing for an interview with a vulnerable or significant witness so that any issues that might arise during this stage of the process can be dealt with.

Interview monitors, camera operators, interpreters, intermediaries, and interview supporters should also be informed about their role as soon as possible. Interpreters and intermediaries must be involved in and actively contribute to the planning process.

10.2.14 **Stage 14: Manage the planning process**

The person/people responsible for the interview strategy should manage the interviewers' preparation of the interview plan. This involves:

- Ensuring that the topics to be covered are detailed, meaningful, and consistent with the objectives;
- Assisting with the structure of the interview;
- Agreeing the general style of the interview (eg use of techniques from the cognitive interview or conversation management);
- Agreeing how the purpose of the interview is to be explained to the witness (need to avoid detail of the alleged offence);
- Agreeing how/whether 'truth and lies' will be dealt with (certain vulnerable witnesses);
- Agreeing the extent and function of rapport building (discussion of neutral topics);
- Agreeing how free narrative is to be 'triggered';
- Agreeing appropriate tactics for dealing with potential barriers to communication;
- Setting out monitoring arrangements (including a means of intervening if necessary).

10.2.15 **Stage 15: Manage witness preparation**

Witnesses should always be prepared for an interview. In some cases, this might be fairly brief and take place immediately prior to the interview, in other instances it might be necessary to take more time and/or for it to take place several hours or days before the interview.

The preparation of the witness should include:

- A developmentally appropriate explanation of the purpose of the interview that does not contain any detail of the alleged offence (eg 'tomorrow we want to talk to you about something that you said to your social worker on Monday', 'tomorrow we want to talk to you about something we think you might have seen in the High Street on Saturday evening');
- The reason for visually recording the interview (eg 'we want to video the interview because it helps us to accurately record what's said and because we might be able to play it as part of your evidence if we go to court');

- The role of the interviewer(s) and anybody else to be present;
- The location of the interview;
- The approximate duration of the interview;
- An explanation of the overall structure of the interview and its ground rules;
- Any issues or concerns raised by the witness (eg welfare issues or concerns about the possibility of intimidation or harassment).

In some instances it might be appropriate to practice the general types of questions that will be asked in the interview by discussing neutral topics.

The evidence should *not* be discussed while preparing a witness for an interview, although any spontaneous comments made by the witness in relation to the alleged offence should be acknowledged and carefully recorded. In either event, a full written record should be made of the preparation of the witness for the interview and the plan for the interview reviewed and revised if necessary.

10.2.16 **Stage 16: Monitor the interview or co-ordinate the interviews**

The person responsible for the interview strategy will usually be involved in either monitoring the interview from the equipment room or, where there is more than one interview, co-ordinating the interviews.

When monitoring the interview, it is important that a means of intervening is agreed with the interviewer beforehand. This might include consultation between the interviewer and the person monitoring the interview during regular breaks, an agreement that the interviewer will consult the person monitoring the interview prior to closing the interview, or monitoring via an earpiece worn by the interviewer. When monitoring the interview it is also important to have a means of communication to the investigative team so that steps can be taken in respect of any information arising from the interview that warrants immediate action.

When coordinating multiple interviews it is important for the person responsible for the interview strategy to set up an effective means of communication between the interview teams and between the interview teams and the investigation team.

10.2.17 **Stage 17: Debrief the interviewers**

The person responsible for the interview strategy should always debrief the interviewers in order to:

- Identify as much information as possible that might assist with the evaluation of the interview (see stage 18 below);
- Identify any welfare issues that need to be addressed.

10.2.18 **Stage 18: Evaluate the interview**

The interview should be evaluated for two reasons:

- To assess the information from the witness in the context of the broader investigation, particularly in terms of:
  - What it tells the investigative team about the alleged event;
  - What fresh lines of inquiry arise from it;
  - Whether there are any gaps in the witness's account;
  - Whether there are any inconsistencies within the witness's account or between the witness's account and other material obtained during the course of the investigation;
- To assess the interviewer's performance with a view to considering:
  - How it might have effected the witness's account;
  - Future interviewer deployments and any developmental needs that might need to be addressed.

10.2.19 **Stage 19: Feedback to the investigating officer/investigating team**

The person responsible for the interview strategy should provide feedback on the interview to the investigating officer or the investigating team at the earliest opportunity.

10.3 **Chapter Summary**

An interview strategy is a high level overview of the interview in the context of the overall investigation. It should not be confused with an interview plan which is more tactical in its composition. A witness interview strategy consists of the following 19 stages:

(1) Review any relevant existing material that is available

(2) Debrief significant others involved in the investigation

(3) Identify investigatively important information

(4) Consider the impact of other investigative strategies on the interview

(5) Identify sources of advice

(6) Assess the witness

(7) Prioritize witness interviews

(8) Set objectives for the interview

(9) Consider the need for and practicality of an 'early special measures meeting' with the Crown Prosecution Service

(10) Identify resources

(11) Consider the timing and location for the interview

(12) Consider what the interviewers are to be told about the offence and case specific investigatively important information in the initial briefing

(13) Brief the interviewers and others involved in the interview process (eg intermediary, interpreter)

(14) Manage the planning process

(15) Manage witness preparation

(16) Monitor the interview or co-ordinate the interviews

(17) Debrief the interviewers

(18) Evaluate the interview

(19) Feedback to the investigating officer/investigating team

SPACE FOR NOTES

SPACE FOR NOTES

SPACE FOR NOTES

Planning and Preparing for Interviews

11.1 **Introduction**

The purpose of an investigative interview with a witness is to establish their account of the matter under investigation and any background information that might assist the investigation team.

11.2 **Information Needed to Plan an Interview**

The planning stage of an interview involves some consideration of three types of information:

(1) Information about the witness;
(2) Information about the alleged offence(s); and
(3) Investigatively important information.

At this stage, interviewers need to have differing amounts of knowledge about each kind of information. In a general sense, they need to know as much about the witness as possible, a little about the alleged offence, and some general knowledge of the investigatively important information relevant to the case.

11.3 **Information About the Witness**

While circumstances can sometimes limit what can be found out about the witness before the interview takes place, a poorly planned interview can have disastrous consequences for an investigation. Interviewers, therefore, need to balance the need to obtain as much information as they can about the witness with their desire to conduct the interview as soon as is practicable.

As much of the following information should be obtained about the witness as possible:

- Age;
- Gender;
- Sexuality (where the alleged offence might contain a homophobic element);
- Race, culture, ethnicity, religion, and first language;
- Preferred name/mode of address;
- The nature and extent of any disabilities or disorders and the implications of this for the interview process;
- Any specialist health and/or mental health needs;
- Any medication being taken and its potential impact on the interview;
- Domestic circumstances (including whether the witness is currently in a 'safe' environment);
- Relationship of the witness to the alleged perpetrator;
- Current emotional state (including trauma, distress, shock, depression, fears of intimidation/recrimination, and recent significant stressful events experienced);

- Likely impact of recalling of traumatic events on the behaviour of the witness;
- Current or previous contact with public services (including previous contact with police, the local adults' services authority, or health professionals);
- Any relevant information or intelligence known.

Where the witness is either a child or has a learning disability, the following information should also be obtained:

- Family members/carers and nature of relationships;
- Routines;
- Any sanctions used with the witness (eg withholding privileges);
- Cognitive abilities (eg memory, attention);
- Linguistic abilities;
- Reaction to authority (eg compliance);
- Sleeping arrangements (if the alleged circumstances relate to abuse in the family or an institutional setting);
- Witness's overall sexual education, knowledge, and experiences (if the alleged circumstances relate to a sexual offence).

The possibility that the witness has experienced discrimination based on race or disability must always be considered and taken into account when planning the interview. Such experience may have a number of different outcomes, including poor self esteem and a distrust of people perceived as having some authority in society.

11.3.1 Pre-interview assessment

In some cases it might be helpful to assess the witness before the interview takes place. Such assessments are usually conducted by interviewers but, in circumstances where there are issues that cannot be readily resolved by contacting carers and professionals already involved with the witness's welfare and there are concerns about the witness's cognitive, emotional, or linguistic functioning, it may be necessary for a specialist to conduct the assessment.

The aim of an assessment should be to supplement the interviewers' knowledge about the witness. The assessment should not aim to discuss the offence since this may subsequently give rise to an allegation of coaching or collusion. Where the witness spontaneously mentions the offence, it should be acknowledged though not pursued.

A pre-interview assessment can take place at the same time as the preparation of the witness for the interview. It could, therefore, include the various aspects of witness preparation such as an explanation of the ground rules of the interview, an outline of the structure of the interview, and the opportunity to practise responding to open-ended questions.

Pre-interview assessment can consist of more than one session if necessary.

A record must be kept of any pre-interview assessment. Such a record is usually written, although it could consist of a video or audio recording where this is thought to be more appropriate.

11.4 Information About the Alleged Offence(s)

Ideally, interviewers should only know little about the alleged offence(s) before the interview. This is so because too much knowledge might result in the interviewer contaminating the interview by:

(a) Inadvertently introducing information that has not already been mentioned by the witness in the interview; and
(b) Not asking all the questions that might otherwise have been asked due to any gaps or a lack of precision in the witness's account being sub-consciously supplemented with prior information about the offence.

It is, therefore, desirable (though not always practical) that such knowledge is confined to:

• The type of alleged offence(s);
• The approximate time and location of the alleged offence(s);
• The scene of the alleged offence(s) (*note*: this should only be enough general knowledge to help the interviewer understand what might be said during the interview); and
• How the alleged offence came to the notice of police.

Where the interviewer is also the investigating officer, has been involved in a multi-agency strategy discussion, or, as a result of circumstances, has needed to interview more than one witness in the case, ABE accepts that he or she is likely to know more about the alleged offence(s) than is ideal. In this situation, interviewers should try as far as possible to avoid contaminating the interview process with their knowledge.

11.5 Investigatively Important Information

In addition to obtaining the witness's account, other matters will often need to be covered during the interview to aid the investigative process. ABE refers to these matters as 'investigatively important information'. Investigatively important information consists of:

• Material relating to general investigative practice; and
• Case specific material.

Where material identified as investigatively important information, either during the planning phase of the interview or during the interview itself is not covered in the witness's account, it may be necessary for the interviewers to deal with it either in the latter part of the questioning phase of the interview or in a further interview, depending on the complexity of the case and the nature of the investigatively important information.

The amount of knowledge that interviewers have about investigatively important information prior to the interview is likely to depend on what they know about the alleged offence. Given that interviewers should ideally know only a little detail of the alleged offence, they will usually know something of the kind of material relating to investigative practice that should be covered in the interview but little if anything about the case specific material relevant to the witness's account. Such case specific material can be made available to the interviewer (from the investigating officer, interview monitor, or the recording equipment operator) at an appropriate point in the interview.

Investigatively important information relating to general investigative practice typically includes:

- Points to prove any offence(s) alleged;
- Information that should be considered when assessing a witness's identification evidence, as suggested in *R v Turnbull and Camelo* ([1976] 63 Cr App R 132) and embodied in the mnemonic ADVOKATE (*Practical Guide to Investigative Interviewing*, published by Centrex, most recent edition 2004):

  A Amount of time under observation

  D Distance from the eyewitness to the person/incident

  V Visibility including time of day, street lighting, etc

  O Obstructions; anything getting in the way of the witness's view

  K Known or seen before; did the witness know, or had he or she seen the alleged perpetrator before?

  A Any reason to remember; was there something specific that made the person/incident memorable?

  T Time lapse; how long since the witness last saw the alleged perpetrator?

  E Errors or material discrepancies

- Anything said by the witness to a third party after the incident (evidence of first complaint etc.);
- Any other witnesses present.

Investigatively important information relating to case specific material typically includes:

- How and where any items used in the commission of the offence were disposed of;
- Any background information relevant to the witness's account (eg matters pertaining to the credibility of the account such as alcohol consumed and/or drugs taken);

- The relationship between the witness and the suspected offender (including the history of the relationship);
- Any risk assessment issues concerning the likely future conduct of the suspected offender;
- Significant evidential inconsistencies between the witness's account and other evidence or information acquired during the investigation;
- Significant evidential omissions from the witness's account.

There are many reasons for significant evidential inconsistencies or omissions and most of them are perfectly innocent. It should, however, be acknowledged that occasions may arise where witnesses can exaggerate or fabricate their account. Whatever the reason for the inconsistency or the omission, it might be necessary to ask the witness about it. In these circumstances, ABE suggests that the following principles should be taken into account:

- Explanations for evidential inconsistencies or omissions should only be sought where the inconsistency is a significant one;
- Explanations for evidential inconsistencies or omissions should only be sought after careful consideration has concluded that there is no obvious explanation for them;
- Explanations for evidential inconsistencies or omissions should only be sought after the witness's account has been fully explored, either at the end of the interview or in a further interview, as appropriate;
- Interviewers should always be aware that the purpose of asking a witness to explain an evidential inconsistency is to establish the truth, it is not to put pressure on a witness to alter their account;
- Questions aimed at eliciting an explanation for an inconsistency or omission should be carefully planned, phrased tactfully, and presented in a non-confrontational manner, and must take account of the extent to which the witness may be vulnerable to suggestion, compliance, or acquiescence.

11.6 **Decision-Making**

There are many different decisions that will need to be considered when embarking on any course of action in relation to interviewing witnesses.

11.6.1 **Whether to interview**

For most witnesses, the decision as to whether to conduct an interview relates to informed consent. In this context, informed consent means that the witness should be in a position to understand the implications of consenting to an interview, specifically, that the record of the interview might be used in criminal, civil, or disciplinary hearings and that they might be required to give evidence.

Witnesses who for any reason cannot understand the implications of consenting to an interview are subject to the procedures discussed in Chapter 7.

11.6.2 **How to record the interview**

The decision as to whether to video the interview with a view to playing it as evidence-in-chief or whether to record it by other means (audio recording or written record) depends on three factors:

1. The availability of video-recorded evidence-in-chief as a special measure in the court in which any trial is likely to take place. This point refers to the phased implementation timetable for the Youth Justice and Criminal Evidence Act 1999 (YJCEA) (see Home Office circulars on the internet for the latest position);
2. For most witnesses who fall within the definitions set down in ss 16 and 17 of the YJCEA, whether the quality of their evidence is likely to be maximized as a result of playing a video-recorded interview as evidence-in-chief. The single exception to this is that child witnesses under 17 to sexual or violent offences are not subject to a consideration about the likely quality of their evidence for the purposes of this special measure and live TV link (s 24). As a result, it is suggested that witnesses to sexual or violent offences who are under 17 *should* be interviewed on video unless insurmountable difficulties are likely to be encountered in doing so;
3. Witnesses do not only have to consent to the interview, they also have to consent to the interview being video-recorded. The effect of this is that some witnesses may consent to being interviewed but might not want that interview to be recorded visually. In these circumstances, the interview will have to be recorded by another means (on audio-tape or in writing). Witnesses who for any reason cannot understand the implications of consenting to the interview being video-recorded are subject to the procedures discussed in Chapter 7.

11.7 **Use of Planning Information**

The planning information should be used to set the objectives for the interview and to determine:

*   The techniques used within the phased interview;
*   The means by which the interview is to be recorded;
*   Who should conduct the interview and if anybody else should be present;
*   Who should monitor the interview (if anybody);
*   Who should operate the equipment;
*   The location of the interview;
*   The timing of the interview;

- The duration of the interview (including pace, breaks, and the possibility of more than one session); and
- What is likely to happen after the interview.

11.8 Objectives

The objectives for the interview should deal with specific issues rather than be framed as general aspirations if they are to aid the planning process: while general aspirations such as 'to establish the truth of the matter under investigation' are fine and laudable aims, they lack the precision needed to structure the interview and focus its direction. The objectives set should focus on time frames, places, and relationships, eg 'to establish the witness's movements on the evening of 6 September', 'to ascertain the witness's account of the events in the High Street on 6 September', 'to obtain the witness's account of the history and nature of her relationship with the suspected offender'.

11.9 Techniques

The kind of techniques used within the phased approach to the interview advocated in ABE depend on what is established at the planning stage and what emerges during the interview itself. For example:

- Some of the techniques developed for the purposes of the cognitive interview might be helpful with a direct eye or ear witness to an event who is able and willing to participate in the process;
- Some of the techniques developed for the purposes of conversation management might be helpful where the witness is less able or willing to participate in the process;
- Where there are concerns that a witness has a learning disability, even if the extent of the disability is considered to be relatively 'mild', it is essential that a great deal of care is taken in framing questions to reduce the possibility of misunderstanding;
- While the recall of traumatic events can cause any witness significant distress, additional sensitivity to the stress likely to be experienced by witnesses with mental disorder might be necessary because of the effect that it might have on their behaviour;
- Witnesses with mental disorder giving rise to delusion might report distorted views or hallucinatory experiences as part of their account. Interviews should probe these accounts sensitively to try and identify what is real and what may be delusional. Direct challenges to the veracity of these experiences could result in extreme reactions and/or distress.

11.10 **Personnel**

11.10.1 **The interviewer**

Consideration should be given as to who is best qualified to lead the interview. The lead interviewer should be a person who:

- Has, or is likely to be able to establish rapport with the witness;
- Understands how to communicate effectively with the witness;
- Understands the rules of evidence;
- Understands the kind of investigatively important information relating to general investigative practice that is relevant to the type of offence being investigated.

In addition to this, the following should be taken into account when deciding who the lead interviewer should be:

- As far as practical, any preference that the witness might have for an interviewer of either gender or sexual orientation or from a particular race, cultural or ethnic background;
- Any personal or domestic issues that a prospective interviewer has that might have an adverse impact on the interview;
- Whether any previous experience that a prospective interviewer has with the witness is likely to either inhibit rapport building or give rise to challenges of coaching, prompting, or offering inducements.

In the case of joint interviews conducted by police and social services either under *Working Together* where the witness is a child or under *No Secrets* (in England) or *In Safe Hands* (in Wales) where the witness is a vulnerable adult the police are responsible for that investigation, including any investigative interview (recommendation 99 of the Victoria Climbié Inquiry Report where the witness is a child). Having responsibility for the criminal investigation does not mean that the police should always take the lead in the investigative interview. Provided both the police officer and the social worker have been adequately trained to conduct interviews in accordance with ABE, there is no reason why either should not lead the interview. In circumstances where a social worker leads the interview, the police should retain their responsibility for the criminal investigation by ensuring that the interview is properly planned and that the police officer has an effective role in monitoring the interview. Similarly, where a police officer leads the interview, the local authority should retain their responsibility for the witness's welfare by ensuring that the interview is properly planned and that the social worker has an effective role in monitoring the interview.

11.10.2 **The interview monitor**

Interview monitors have an important role in ensuring that:

- The interview is conducted in a professional manner;
- The witness's needs are kept paramount;
- Any gaps in the witness's account are identified and addressed.

Consideration should be given as to whether the interview monitor is present in the interviewing room itself (in the event of which he or she might effectively be regarded as being a 'second interviewer'), or in the adjoining room with the monitoring equipment (in which case he or she might effectively be regarded as being an 'observer'). The possibility that the witness might feel intimidated by the presence of too many people in the interview room should be taken into account in determining where an interview monitor is situated, particularly where an interview supporter and interpreter are also to be present in the interview room.

11.10.3 **Equipment operators**

Somebody should always be identified to operate the recording equipment throughout the interview so that the view recorded by the camera can be adjusted if the witness moves and any equipment failure can be identified at the earliest possible moment.

11.11 **Support**

There are many different types of supporters. These will range from someone who offers emotional support to the interpreter who assists with language barriers, and the more complex role of the intermediary.

11.11.1 **Interpreters**

Witnesses should be interviewed in the language of their choice, unless every effort to secure an interpreter for that language has proved unsuccessful. While this will usually be their first language, circumstances may arise where it is more appropriate to use a second language. Where a sexual offence is involved, some witnesses may use their first language to describe intimate concepts even though they appear fluent in English. For this reason, the possibility of using an interpreter should be considered even where a witness is bilingual.

Interpreters should be appropriately trained and accredited. Family members or other close relatives should not be used because it is important that interpreters are seen to be independent, impartial, and unbiased.

It is essential that interpreters are involved in the planning process. Interpreters are trained to translate for meaning because some words in English do not have an exact equivalent in other languages. An understanding of the objectives of the interview, its structure and, importantly, the function served by specific interview techniques, such as those that make up the cognitive interview, could prove crucial to the interpreter being able to effectively discharge this function.

If the witness does not communicate by speech, an interpreter capable of signing may be required. In many instances, the type of sign language used is likely to be British Sign Language (BSL). Where BSL is used, it is important to establish which regional dialect the witness is familiar with since this can be the source of some confusion. While BSL is certainly the most common form of sign language, it should be noted that it is not the only form of sign language. There are many other forms of sign language including Northern Irish Sign Language, Irish Sign Language, Australian Sign Language, American Sign Language, Sign Supported English (SSE), Paget Gorman, and Signed English. Makaton signs and Signalong are sometimes used by people with learning disabilities: where these communication systems are being used, an intermediary rather than an interpreter should be considered.

Where a signer is being used, a camera should be used to record the signer's hand movements as well as those of the witness. In these circumstances, it will often be necessary to secure additional recording equipment.

Where a signer is to be used, it is important to remember that the energy involved in signing is such that the hands of the signer and the witness are likely to get tired. The interview plan should take account of this by:

- Building in the need for breaks to give the signer and the witness an opportunity to rest their hands;
- Considering the possibility of using two signers so that they can either act alternately or in relay.

11.11.2 Intermediaries

What is an intermediary?

Intermediaries are professional people who have developed the skills necessary to communicate effectively with various groups of vulnerable witnesses. They include speech and language therapists, clinical psychologists, psychiatric nurses, teachers, special needs school teachers, and social workers. An Intermediary Registration Board (IRB) has been established by the Office for Criminal Justice Reform (OCJR). The IRB oversees registration of intermediaries and their standards. Registered intermediaries are accredited by the IRB and the OCJR following a selection and training process assessed against a set of core competencies required for the intermediary role.

Who is eligible for an intermediary?

'Vulnerable' witnesses as defined by s 16 of the YJCEA 1999 are eligible for an intermediary where it is likely that this particular special measure will maximize the quality of their evidence. 'Intimidated' witnesses as defined by s 17 of the Act are not eligible for an intermediary.

The effect of this is that younger child witnesses and witnesses of any age who are vulnerable by virtue of a disability that has an adverse impact on their ability to communicate could benefit from an intermediary at the time of the interview and, subsequently, while giving evidence in court. The circumstances where it may be appropriate to consider an intermediary include:

- Where the witness is a younger child (eg pre-school or early primary school);
- Where the witness is a child who has a delay in the development of their language;
- Where the witness has sustained an injury that has an impact on their ability to communicate, for example:
  - A blow to the head, the neck, or the jaw;
  - An injury that affects the witness's ability to breath freely;
  - Any injury resulting in the need for a medical intervention that has an effect on the witness's ability to communicate such as a tracheotomy;
  - An injury to the brain as a result of a medical condition such as a stroke giving rise to dysphasia;
- Where the witness has a learning disability that has an impact on their ability to communicate. This is likely to include circumstances where the extent of the witness's disability might not always be immediately apparent (eg Asperger's Syndrome);
- Where the witness has a mental illness that impacts on their ability to give a coherent account. This is likely to include conditions giving rise to distorted or delusional thinking.

In brief, an intermediary may be able to help improve the quality of evidence of any vulnerable witness who is unable to detect and cope with misunderstanding, or to clearly express their answers to questions in the context of an interview or while giving evidence in court.

How do intermediaries work in practice?

At the time of writing, access to the intermediary register was via the OCJR, although it is understood that responsibility for its day-to-day management may rest elsewhere in the future. Up to date information on how to access the intermediary register is set out in the *Intermediary Procedural Guidance Manual* that is published by the OCJR.

Access to the intermediary register begins by the completion of a form in which the communication needs of the witness are specified. The communication needs of the witness are then matched against the skills of the intermediaries on the register with a view to identifying the most appropriate intermediary for the witness.

Before an intermediary can assist with communication they need to conduct one or more assessment meetings with the witness. The purpose of this assessment is:

- To establish whether the intermediary can communicate effectively with the witness (an intermediary might conclude that effective communication cannot reliably be established or that another person is better placed to communicate with the witness);
- To enable the intermediary to assess the witness's communication needs, devise strategies, and make recommendations as to how to maximize understanding;
- To give the intermediary an opportunity to build a rapport with the witness and to determine whether they are the right person to act as an intermediary.

Details of what is alleged to have been witnessed are not discussed during assessment meetings but it is accepted that the witness might make spontaneous comments about the alleged event. For this reason, an intermediary should never be left alone with a witness: a responsible third party, such as a social worker or a police officer, should always be present.

The extent to which the intermediary is actively involved in the communication of questions and answers during the interview varies from witness to witness, depending on their particular needs and communication style.

Even though the Youth Justice and Criminal Evidence Act 1999 says that an intermediary can assist a vulnerable witness to communicate by explaining questions put to and answers given by them, this happens rarely in practice. It is more common for intermediaries to contribute to the process by:

- Helping to plan the interview by providing advice on how questions should be asked;
- Intervening during the interview where miscommunication is likely by helping the interviewer to rephrase questions or by repeating the witness's answers where they might otherwise be inaudible or unclear on the recording.

The use of an unregistered person as intermediary can only be considered once the options for using a registered intermediary have been exhausted. When an unregistered intermediary is used they must be independent of the case being investigated. There is a preference for unregistered intermediaries to be professional people rather than family members, friends, or associates. In the event that the particular circumstances of the case are such that it appears that only a non-professional person can perform the function of an intermediary, it is important that the witness is assessed by a registered intermediary before proceeding in order to confirm that the role can only be performed by the non-professional. A briefing pack to be used by unregistered intermediaries setting out the role of the intermediary is available from the OCJR.

Discussions with the intermediary at the planning stage should include the arrangements for leading the interview, legal and confidentiality requirements, and the exact role that the intermediary will take. The potentially explicit nature of the topics to be covered should be addressed. The intermediary should be provided with information that is relevant to their role and will help them to maximize communication/understanding (eg the specific vocabulary used by the witness and relevant relationships).

Some witnesses with physical or learning disabilities communicate using a mixture of words and other communication systems that include signing and/or the use of symbol systems. In these circumstances, signs and symbols are said to be used as augmentative communication systems. Some witnesses with physical or learning disabilities do not use speech at all but communicate by signing and/or using symbol systems. In these circumstances, signs and symbols are said to be used as an alternative communication system. Examples of sign systems include Makaton signing and Signalong. Examples of symbol systems include Rebus, Bliss, and Makaton symbols. The symbols may be printed onto boards or cards, or contained in booklets. They vary from being iconic and concrete to being more abstract in their composition. They may be personalized and can be composed of words, pictures, and symbols. The services of an intermediary are essential in circumstances where a witness uses an augmentative or an alternative method of communication.

11.11.3 Aids to communication

'Vulnerable' witnesses as defined by s 16 of the YJCEA are eligible for aids to communication where it is likely that this particular special measure will maximise the quality of their evidence. 'Intimidated' witnesses as defined by s 17 of the Act are not eligible for aids to communication.

Aids to communication include:

- Computers or other electronic communication equipment;
- Communication boards or books composed of letters or symbols.

These aids to communication can be used by a variety of means including fingers pressing the keys on a keyboard, a tube connected to a computer that moves a cursor around when the witness blows into it, or other means of moving a cursor around such as the witness manipulating a joystick with their chin. The symbols on a communication board or in a communication book can be indicated by pointing to them or by blinking. An intermediary must always be considered where aids to communication are used.

11.11.4 **Interview supporters**

Witnesses may have a supporter during the interview for the purposes of pre-trial preparation and/or during the trial itself. This section deals exclusively with the interview supporter although the role of a supporter at other stages of the criminal justice process should not be forgotten.

It can be helpful for a person who is known to the witness to be present during the interview. The role of such an 'interview supporter' is primarily one of emotional support, although they may also be able to contribute towards the planning process with additional information about the communication needs of the witness. Wherever possible the views of the witness should be established prior to the interview as to whether they want a supporter present during the interview and, if so, who this should be.

Interview supporters must be independent of the case. This point excludes the following from acting as interview supporters:

- Other witnesses, including those giving evidence of an early complaint;
- People alleged to be involved in the offence in some way (either in terms of its commission or in terms of any perceived negligence in failing to protect the witness);
- Interpreters or intermediaries.

In some circumstances using a person who is well-known to the witness as an interview supporter can prove counter-productive by inhibiting the disclosure of information. This may arise as a result of:

- Embarrassment stemming from sensitive information being disclosed in the presence of a person seen by the witness on a day-to-day basis;
- Stress stemming from the disclosure of unpleasant information that the witness thinks is likely to upset the potential supporter.

For this reason, the potential impact of the witness's relationship with the supporter on the interview process should be taken into account. Carers can, however, wait in an adjacent room if it is thought that physical proximity might be helpful to the witness.

In every case, interview supporters should be fully briefed that their role is limited to providing emotional support and that they must not prompt or speak for the witness. Interview supporters should be asked to consider carefully how best to comfort the witness if they become distressed. While the witness should be reassured, it may not be appropriate to physically touch them because some vulnerable witnesses might perceive this as an invasion of personal space or even as abusive.

11.12 **Location**

Active consideration should be given to the location of the interview and the layout of the room in which it is to take place.

While planning the interview the interviewer should try to find out where the witness would prefer to be interviewed. While the controlled environment of a purpose built interview suite is usually the preferred option from an interviewer's point of view, some witnesses might prefer to be interviewed in a setting familiar and comfortable to them. Whatever the case, the location should be quiet enough to avoid a situation in which background noise is likely to interfere with the quality of the sound on any video or audio recording, free from interruptions, free from distractions, and free from fear and intimidation.

Where witnesses are interviewed at their home address, care should be taken to avoid saying anything or visually recording any background material that might lead to the location being identified (the use of background screens should be considered if necessary).

Wherever the interview takes place, pens and paper should be available for use where a witness's recall could be assisted by drawing a sketch or plan. Any such sketches or plans drawn in the interview must be retained as exhibits.

Toys and play materials can be used where they might assist with rapport building or in helping the witness to give their account more effectively. Care should be taken not to use toys or play materials in a leading manner and some thought should be given to the potential that they have for leading the witness when selecting them during the planning phase. Toys and play materials should be stored out of sight, to minimize the potential that they have for distracting the witness, and only brought out where necessary. Any toys and play materials used should be developmentally, culturally and gender appropriate.

11.13 **Timing**

While the interview will usually take place as soon after an allegation emerges as is practicable, rushing to conduct an interview, without proper planning, can be counter-productive. The following should be considered when determining the timing of an interview:

- The witness's routines. Interviewers should avoid starting an interview just before a mealtime or at any time when the witness is likely to be tired (eg just before they usually go to bed);
- The effects of any medication taken by the witness. For example, taking some slow release medicines will result in the witness being tired by the afternoon;
- The potential effects of trauma and/or stress. Trauma and stress can interfere with the process of remembering but this should be determined by asking the witness rather than by the imposition of an arbitrary period of time. Some witnesses will want to be interviewed relatively quickly while others might

wish to be interviewed at a later date. It should always be borne in mind that the potential for memory contamination taking place increases over time.

In the event of circumstances being such that it is absolutely essential for witnesses to be interviewed at a time when they are tired (for example, where an alleged offender is in police custody for a serious offence and an interview is necessary to secure potentially vital evidence) a brief interview can take place that sets out the witness's account and addresses any issues on which immediate action needs to be taken. A more substantial interview can then be arranged at an appropriate time.

11.14 **Duration**

It helps the interviewer and the witness to have an idea of approximately how long each interview is likely to last. Estimates of the number of interviews likely to be needed and their approximate duration should take account of the following:

- What is known about the witness's communication skills and intellectual functioning;
- The likely effect of any disabilities on the witness's behaviour in the interview;
- The likely effect of any health or mental health issues on the witness's behaviour in the interview;
- What is known about the witness's emotional condition;
- How much time is likely to be needed to establish rapport;
- The number and complexity of the alleged incidents to be described.

In some circumstances it might be necessary to conduct the interview over more than one session. These sessions might be separated by a matter of hours or, if necessary, could take place over a number of days. When this occurs, care must be taken to avoid repetition of the same focused questions over time, which could lead to unreliable or inconsistent responding in some witnesses and interviews being ruled inadmissible by the court.

Many witnesses with a learning disability will be unable to give their evidence in one long interview. In many instances, several short interviews, preferably though not necessarily held on the same day, would be more likely to lead to a satisfactory outcome. Some witnesses with health or mobility issues may similarly benefit from several short interviews.

When planning the interview, interviewers should obtain advice from people who know the witness about the likely length of time that they can be interviewed before a pause or break is offered. Breaks should be offered or taken during the interview in accordance with this information.

11.15 Preparation of the Witness and Their Carers for an Interview

11.15.1 Witnesses

Witnesses should always be prepared for an interview. In some cases, this might be fairly brief and take place immediately prior to the interview. Where the quality of communication with the witness is likely to benefit from extensive rapport building, such as is often the case with some young child witnesses and witnesses with learning disabilities or mental health issues, it might be necessary to take more time so that preparation takes place several hours or days before the interview.

Some witnesses may benefit from a familiarization visit to the interview suite as part of the preparation process.

The preparation of the witness for the interview should address the following in a manner appropriate to the witness's understanding:

- An explanation of the purpose of the interview and the reason for visually recording it (including who might subsequently view it);
- The role of the interviewer(s) and anybody else to be present;
- The location of the interview and approximately how long it is likely to take;
- The general structure of the interview;
- The ground rules applicable to the interview, including:
  - That the witness can ask for a break at any time during the interview (it might be necessary to agree a signal for this where the witness uses an alternative method of communication);
  - That the witness should not make any assumptions about the interviewer's knowledge of the event;
  - That the witness should tell the interviewer if the interviewer asks a question they do not understand;
  - That the witness should tell the interviewer if a question they do not know the answer to is asked;
  - That the witness should tell the interviewer if the interviewer says something (eg in the form of a question or a summary) that suggests that they have misunderstood what the witness has said;
- Where the witness's understanding of truth and lies is to be explored (eg witnesses under 17 and some witnesses with learning disabilities), the purpose of this procedure should be explained.

11.15.2 Carers

Carers should be told that witnesses should never be offered inducements for co-operating with the investigative process.

If the witness makes any spontaneous comments about the alleged offence or any other offence, the carer should be asked to:

- Record what was said, where and when it was said and who was present as soon as possible;
- Acknowledge that what the witness said is important and reassure them if they are concerned or distressed but not discuss it any further;
- Report what was said to a member of the investigative team at the earliest opportunity.

The carer should also be asked to similarly record, respond to, and report anything said to them by anybody else involved in the case.

Carers should also be given information about what further role, if any, they may have in planning the interview or in being present while it is conducted (or given reasons why the interviewers would prefer them not to be present).

Any issues or concerns raised by the witness or their carers should be addressed while preparing them for the interview (for example, welfare issues or concerns about the possibility of a later court appearance).

Full written notes must be kept of the preparation of a witness for an interview and revealed to the CPS.

The information obtained to plan the interview should be reviewed and revised if necessary in the light of any additional information that arises from preparing the witness for the interview.

11.15.3 **Early special measures meetings**

A pre-interview early special measures meeting should be considered in all cases other than where the only decision to be made is whether to video the interview or not and the decision to video-record the interview is a foregone conclusion (eg there is little point in calling a pre-interview early special measures meeting solely for the purposes of deciding whether to video the interview or not in circumstances where the primary rule applies [child witnesses in sexual or violent cases], unless there are the kind of 'insurmountable difficulties' to video recording that are mentioned in Vol 1 of ABE).

Unless it is impractical to do so, a pre-interview early special measures meeting should take place where:

- There is any doubt as to whether to video-record the interview;
- An intermediary or aids to communication are involved;
- There might be an issue about somebody that the witness requests as a supporter for the purposes of the interview.

Police investigators are responsible for calling an early special measures meeting during the investigation, where this is necessary. These meetings are, in practice, usually telephone discussions, the decisions of which are recorded on the form in Annex A of *Early Special Measures Meetings between the Police and the Crown Prosecution Service and Meetings between the Crown Prosecution Service and Vulnerable or Intimidated Witnesses* (Home Office, 2001).

11.15.4 Record of the planning process

A written record must be made of the decisions made during the planning process and of reasons for them. This record should be referred to in the Criminal Justice Act 1967 statement subsequently made by the interviewer about the interview process and should be revealed to the CPS under the requirements of the Criminal Procedure and Investigations Act 1996.

11.16 Chapter Summary

The planning stage of an interview involves some consideration of three types of information:

(1) Information about the witness;
(2) Information about the alleged offence(s); and
(3) Investigatively important information.

Interviewers need to have differing amounts of knowledge about each kind of information during the planning stage. In a general sense, they need to know as much about the witness as possible, a little about the alleged offence, and some general knowledge of the investigatively important information relevant to the case.

This information should then be used to make decisions as to:

• Whether to interview;
• How to record any interview.

If a decision is made to proceed with the interview, the planning information should be used to determine the:

• Objectives;
• Techniques;
• Personnel;
• Support;
• Location;
• Timing; and
• Duration of the interview.

All witnesses and carers should be prepared for the interview. More extensive preparation is likely to be necessary where the witness is a young child, has learning disabilities or mental health issues.

SPACE FOR NOTES

SPACE FOR NOTES

12

Conducting Interviews

12.1 **Introduction**

Interviews with witnesses should normally consist of the following phases:

ABE	PEACE
Planning and preparation	Planning and preparation
Establishing rapport	Engage and explain
Initiating and supporting a free narrative account	Account, clarification, and challenge
Questioning	
Closing the interview	Closure
Evaluation	Evaluation

It is important to understand that these are frameworks for interviewing, rather than models, in the sense that they are the structures within which specific techniques are used.

It is also important to understand that the framework described in *Achieving Best Evidence* (ABE) is entirely compatible with the PEACE framework advocated by the Association of Chief Police Officers (ACPO, 2007).

Chapter 11 dealt with planning and preparation, this chapter sets out to describe the phases of the interview itself.

12.2 **Rapport**

The rapport phase can be regarded as consisting of three elements:

• Formalities;
• Ground rules;
• Neutral topics.

12.2.1 **Formalities**

This element of the rapport phase contains the following:

• Anybody in the interview suite should be introduced to the witness before the commencement of the interview. This includes equipment operators and any other people in the control room viewing the interview.
• Where a supporter, such as a carer, has accompanied the witness to an interview suite, but is not going to be present during the interview, the witness should be shown where the supporter will wait.
• The recording equipment should be checked to ensure that it is in working order.
• The recording equipment should be checked to ensure that it is switched on.

- The main Pan Tilt Zoom (PTZ) camera should be aligned and focused so that it records a picture of the witness from just above the top of their head to either their waist or their knees (depending on posture).
- Any additional PTZ cameras that are being used to record such details as a signer's hand movements or the use of an aid to communication such as a communication board should be aligned and focused as appropriate.
- The interviewer should state the day, date, time, and place or, where it might be helpful to demonstrate the witness's level of understanding, ask the witness to do so.
- All present should be asked to introduce themselves.
- The roles of all present should be briefly explained to the witness for the purposes of the recording.
- The presence and location of the cameras and their function as a permanent record of the interview should be pointed out.
- The reason for the interview should be stated in a way that makes its focus clear but does not specify the nature of the offence.
- It should be explained that the interviewer might take a few *brief* notes, where applicable.

12.2.2 **Ground rules**

This element of the rapport phase contains the following:

- An explanation of the following ground rules:
  - That the interviewer is relying on the witness's account, because they were not present when the events under investigation took place;
  - That the witness should try to give as detailed account as possible;
  - That the witness should say so if they do not know the answer to a question asked by the interviewer;
  - That the witness should say so if they do not understand a question asked by the interviewer;
  - That the witness should say so if the interviewer says something (eg in the form of a summary or a question) that suggests he or she has misunderstood what the witness says.
- The interviewer should tell the witness that they can ask for a break at any time.
- The interviewer should explore the witness's understanding of truth and lies where this is appropriate. Such an exploration of truth and lies is appropriate where:
  - The witness is under 17;
  - The witness has a moderate, severe, or profound learning disability.

- Where it is appropriate to explore the witness's understanding of truth and lies:
  - The witness should be told the purpose of asking them about truth and lies in order to allay any suspicion that it is a challenge to their integrity (for example, 'I need to ask you some questions about truth and lies because it's important in these kind of interviews for us to be able to demonstrate to the court that you understand what truth and lies are').
  - Less able witnesses should be presented with an example in the form of a scenario in which one of the characters intends to deceive another by means of a lie and asked to comment on it. The scenario should then be altered so that the character tells the truth and the witness should be asked to comment on that. ABE provides examples of these kinds of scenarios in Chapter 2, 'Planning and Conducting Interviews with Children', although interviewers can use any scenario provided that it includes overt deception on the part of one of the characters.
  - More able witnesses should be asked to explain the difference between truth and lies by providing their own examples. Where the examples or explanations given by the witness do not include an overt element of deception, the interviewer will need to probe the witness's understanding of truth and lies.

12.2.3 Neutral topics

A discussion of neutral topics such as the witness's hobbies or interests should never amount to a mechanical process aimed at ticking an item off a mental script of the interview formulated by the interviewer. It is an important aspect of the rapport phase that can serve two functions:

1. To help the witness and the interviewer relax and feel as comfortable as possible;
2. Where appropriate, to provide the witness with an introduction into the style of questions that will be asked and to help the witness get accustomed to the amount of detail in their answers that the interviewer will need.

The extent to which neutral topics are discussed very much depends on the witness: some witnesses, particularly those who are very young or have a learning disability, will need more time to get to know the interviewer and become familiar with the style of interaction than others.

A developmentally appropriate explanation should always be given for discussing neutral topics to avert a situation in which a witness who thinks that they have come to the interview to talk about the alleged offence is suddenly baffled when non-offence information is introduced by the interviewer.

12.3 **Free Narrative Account**

12.3.1 **Initiating free narrative**

The way in which an interviewer endeavours to initiate free narrative very much depends on the witness and on how the alleged offence came to the notice of the investigators.

In many instances, the witness will have already made a complaint to another person (eg a carer, a teacher, a social worker, or a police officer). In these instances, it may be appropriate to initiate free narrative by referring to the fact that that complaint was made. It is important to remember here that the reference to the complaint should not go into detail because that might be construed as leading. An appropriate example might be 'as I said earlier (in the formalities to the rapport phase) the reason for this interview is that we want to you to tell us about what you said to your mum yesterday about what happened in school on Monday. Please tell us about that'.

In other instances, the witness might not have previously told anybody about the offence. In these cases, initiating free narrative can obviously be a challenge but it is by no means an insurmountable problem. The method used to try to initiate a free narrative account very much depends on what the witness is alleged to have experienced. For example, where abuse is suspected within a particular setting (such as the home or an institutional environment), it may be appropriate to ask the witness to tell the interviewer about the routines in that setting and to describe them in ever increasing detail. Where abuse is suspected to have been committed by a particular individual, it may be appropriate to explore the relationship between that individual and the witness, beginning with the general nature of the relationship in the context of other relationships and gradually exploring it in ever increasing detail.

12.3.2 **Supporting free narrative**

Having initiated free narrative, it is necessary to support it to get the most from the witness's account. The less an interviewer speaks during this phase the better because it is important that the witness's account remains uncontaminated. Interviewers should not interrupt or intervene in any way that forces the witness to change topic.

Free narrative accounts, however, do often need to be supported and encouraged. This may be done by:

- Non-verbal behaviour demonstrating listening on the part of the interviewer. This is likely to include such posture, orientation, and eye-contact in a matter that takes account of the witness's particular needs;

- Simple verbal behaviour such as 'mm';
- Verbal prompts such as:
  - Echoing what the witness has said;
  - Asking simple open-ended questions such as 'what happened next?' and 'is there anything else you can tell me?'.

12.4 **Questioning**

After the free narrative account phase of the interview and before asking questions, interviewers should let the witness know that they are going to ask them some questions in order to expand and clarify what they have said, and remind the witness of the following ground rules:

- That the witness should say so if they do not know the answer to a question asked by the interviewer;
- That the witness should say so if they do not understand a question asked by the interviewer;
- That the witness should say so if the interviewer says something (eg in the form of a summary or a question) that suggests he or she has misunderstood what the witness has said;
- The interviewer should tell the witness that they can ask for a break at any time.

The interviewer should then divide the witness's account into manageable topics, and probe those topics in the order in which the witness presented them during their account (this might not be in a chronological order).

Each topic should be probed by asking the witness to report it again in as much depth as possible (for example, 'to help me really understand what you told me, it would really help me if you tell me again, in as much detail as possible, everything that happened from the time you entered the park to the time the man jumped out from behind the tree').

This should be done systematically by probing each topic beginning by asking open-ended questions before moving on to closed specific questions. These questions should:

- Be simple;
- Only contain one point each;
- Make use of the words/concepts that the witness is familiar with (eg for time, location, persons);
- Avoid the use of jargon and, unless the witness is familiar with them, abstract concepts;
- Not contain double negatives.

These question types and other more restricted types of question are described below. It is acknowledged that, over the years, different authors have classified questions in different ways and that the social and linguistic context in which a question is asked exerts an influence on how it will be interpreted by the listener. This book, however, makes use of the definitions of particular types of question as set out in the revised edition of ABE.

The exploration of each topic should be complete before moving on to the next topic: interviewers should avoid what ABE refers to as 'topic hopping'. Changes in topic should be clearly marked by the interviewer (for example, 'I'd now like to move on to what happened when the man jumped out from behind the tree').

12.4.1 Open-ended questions

Open-ended questions are those worded so as to encourage the witness to provide an unrestricted response. Questions beginning with the words 'tell', 'explain', or 'describe' tend to be typical of this type of question (open-ended questions are sometimes referred to as TED questions for this reason).

12.4.2 Specific-closed

Specific-closed questions are those worded in a way that narrows down the range of responses that the interviewer intends to elicit from a witness. These questions are typically (though by no means exclusively) those beginning with the words 'where', 'what', 'when, 'why', and 'how' (specific-closed questions are sometimes referred to as 5WH questions for this reason). It is important to note that questions beginning with 'why' can sometimes be construed by witnesses as blaming them for something that happened or do not happen (for example, 'Why didn't you tell anybody about this?'). 'Why' questions should, therefore, be avoided whenever possible. Where it is not possible to avoid a 'why' question, it should be framed and asked with considerable care.

12.4.3 Forced-choice questions

Forced-choice questions are those that contain a limited number of alternative responses. These questions should only be used where the circumstances demand it: some witnesses with learning and physical disabilities may find it difficult to respond to anything other than a forced-choice question. Where it is necessary to ask a forced-choice question, it is best to avoid asking those with only two alternatives as a means of reducing the potential that these kind of questions can have for leading the witness (for example, 'were the lights on or were they off or don't you know?'). ABE points out that if it is essential to ask forced-choice questions consisting of only two alternatives they should be phrased in such a way that 'they sometimes result in the first alternative being chosen and sometimes in the second alternative' as a means of ensuring that the witness is not simply responding by rote to the position of the alternative in the question.

Where, as a result of disability, a witness can only respond 'yes' or 'no' to a question it is essential that the services of an intermediary are secured and that the interview is planned with the utmost care.

12.4.4 Multiple questions

Multiple questions are those that ask about several things at the same time. They are easiest to detect when they are framed as a series of questions rapidly following each other before the witness is able to respond (for example, *'What did the car look like? When did you first see it? Where did it go to?'*). Less obvious examples of multiple questions are those that refer to multiple features of the witness's account such as 'what did they look like?'.

Multiple questions should be avoided because they confuse the witness by encouraging them to focus on multiple aspects of their account simultaneously, and because they are of little value to the interviewer as it is not always clear what question has and what question has not been answered, giving rise to a need for further clarification.

12.4.5 Leading questions

There are two kinds of leading questions:

1. Questions that imply the answer;
2. Questions that assume facts likely to be disputed.

Questions that imply the answer are those that hint at the answer the interviewer is looking for. The most common examples of this type of question are those with a 'tag' such as 'that must have hurt, didn't it?'.

Questions that assume facts likely to be in dispute are usually those containing information that has been introduced into the interview by the interviewer, rather than by the witness. Questions such as these can be quite subtle, for example, the question 'was he wearing a hat?' might be considered leading where a witness has not already mentioned it. It is not invariably the case, however, that information introduced into the interview by the interviewer will be considered leading. Where a fact is unlikely to be in dispute such as the presence of a mark on a victim's arm, it may be perfectly permissible for an interviewer to ask 'how did you get that mark?' (at an appropriate point in the interview), without the witness having mentioned it first (while the nature of the mark may be open to dispute, its presence is unlikely to be challenged where there is medical and/or photographic evidence).

Where it is essential that a leading question is put to a witness (for example, where it is imperative that an inconsistency or omission is clarified and it cannot be addressed in any other way), the question should be framed in a way that leads as little as possible (in terms of wording and content) and it should be followed by an open-ended question where the witness's response contains an evidentially relevant material.

12.5 **Closing the Interview**

Interviewers should avoid ending an interview abruptly. In the closure phase of the interview interviewers should:

- Check with the interview monitor and anybody else present either in the interview room or in a monitoring room that everything that needs to be covered in the interview has been covered;
- Summarize the evidentially important statements made by the witness, using the witness's own words as far as possible;
- Answer any questions that the witness has;
- Ask the witness to make a written note of anything else that they remember about the incident in the future and tell them to contact the investigating team (if this is not appropriate, as a result age or disability, the interviewer should ask the witness's carer to do this after the interview);
- Provide advice on seeking help and a contact number;
- Return to rapport or other neutral topics;
- Thank the witness for their time and effort;
- Report the end-time of the interview;
- Record a Victim Personal Statement on the same recording, following a clear break, where this is appropriate.

12.6 **Evaluation**

There are two aspects to evaluating an interview:

1. Evaluation of the information obtained;
2. Evaluation of the interviewer's performance.

Evaluation of the information obtained includes an assessment of:

- What information has been obtained;
- How the account given fits in with other available evidence;
- Whether any action needs to be taken;
- What further inquiries need to be made in respect of the matter being investigated.

The interviewer's skills should be evaluated either in the form of a self-assessment or by a supervisor. In either event, areas of good and poor performance should be identified and incorporated into a development plan.

12.7 **Chapter Summary**

Interviews conducted in accordance with ABE consist of a number of phases that are entirely compatible with the PEACE model advocated by the Association of Chief Police Officers (ACPO).

The ABE framework consists of the following:

- Planning and preparation (see Chapter 11);
- Rapport:
  - Formalities
  - Ground rules
  - Neutral topics
- Free Narrative Account:
  - Initiating free narrative
  - Supporting free narrative
- Questioning:
  - Ground rules
  - Topic division and selection
  - Open-ended questions
  - Specific-closed questions
- Closing the interview
- Evaluating the interview.

Forced-choice, multiple, and leading questions have also been discussed.

SPACE FOR NOTES

SPACE FOR NOTES

SPACE FOR NOTES

13

Storage and Retention of Recordings

13.1 **Introduction**

Once an investigator has completed their visually recorded statement with the vulnerable adult or child witness, there are still several matters that will need to be attended to in respect of the recorded medium. The interview process will result in the production of two or more tapes or discs which will have been produced simultaneously during the interview process.

One of the recordings (normally the top VHS tape, CD, or DVD) will need to be designated as the master recording of the interview.

The reason for this is that the master recording will be sealed to retain its integrity. The master recording of the interview will need to be sealed in the presence of the child or vulnerable adult and their carer or supporter immediately it is taken out of the recording equipment. It will need to be signed by the interviewee and if necessary counter-signed by the parent or carer. It will also need to be signed by the person conducting the interview and any other person present as well as the equipment operator.

13.2 **Documentation**

At the end of the interview process, the interview team will have several items of documentation to complete. The first thing that will need to be done is to seal the designated master recording using a self-adhesive seal that has been specifically designed for this purpose. Each seal will normally bear its own unique identification number consisting of a series of letters and numbers.

The next task that must be completed is that a record should be made in a video-interview movement log. The interview movement log should be updated with the number of recordings that have been produced as part of the interview process. The movement log should also be updated periodically to reflect the fact that further copies have been made including the location of such recordings. The system should be such that a record is kept of all movements of the recordings (eg for purposes of viewing, for copying, or for editing).

Prior to delivering the recording by hand to the CPS, the movement log should be updated to reflect the fact that the interview recording is now no longer at the police station, but has been transferred to the CPS.

Failure to complete a movement log and to keep it updated with the production and location of all recordings will mean that at the conclusion of any proceedings investigators will not know how many recordings have to be recovered and who or where from. Identifying the location and arranging the collection of recordings at the conclusion of the case is the responsibility of the officer in the case. Having done this, the movement log will need to be updated to reflect the fact that all the recordings have been returned.

At the end of the recording process, the controller will also be required to complete a pro forma style location statement. This statement should include the type and amount of equipment used (number and purpose of cameras, number of microphones), the location of the interview, date, time, persons present, and their roles.

13.2.1 **Movement**

If an advice or case file is completed by the police, and the case papers are sent to the CPS, the interview recording must then be taken to the CPS by hand, and a written receipt must be obtained from the CPS representative who takes receipt of the recording from the investigator. This receipt must be filed and retained with the relevant entry in the interview movement log. Prior to delivering the recording to the CPS, investigators will need to update the movement log to reflect the fact that the interview disc is now no longer at the police station, but has been transferred to the CPS. Recordings should always be delivered by hand due to the sensitive nature of the information contained on the recording.

It also follows that if a recording is removed from its storage location for viewing by either the witness or a member of another agency, the movement log should be updated to show who removed it, who viewed it, and which organization they represent, and when it was viewed.

13.2.2 **Additional copies**

Any additional recordings that are either produced at the time of the interview or copied subsequently for any court hearings or for advice files for the CPS will be known as working copies. All versions either master or working copies will need to be treated with great care. They should be stored in a secure cabinet that is designated specifically for the task and kept there unless they are being viewed or have been taken out for service on the defence by the CPS or in certain cases the civil court. If the case then goes to trial, extra copies of the interview disc will be required by the CPS, one copy for the court and one each per defendant. If, after an agency has been supplied with a copy of the recording, they state they have misplaced their copy, they should not automatically be supplied with a further copy without authority or proof of misplacement.

13.2.3 **Managing the consumables**

In view of their expense, it is important to have a system in place which enables investigators to account for the recording media. It is therefore important that the person booking out the blank recording media and associated documentation is able to provide a crime reference or other reference number to show against the allocation of these items at the time of booking.

13.3 **Access to Recordings**

Officers will mainly need to be able to gain access to recordings in order to view them, or facilitate their viewing, or to make further copies. Access to the recordings will need to be strictly controlled in order to preserve the integrity of the recording, and for reasons of confidentiality. Officers needing access to recordings are required to sign for the recording prior to its removal from storage.

13.3.1 **Viewing the recordings**

Investigating or interviewing officers may need to view the visually recorded statement to review the evidential content of the interview itself. Other professionals who are involved in the case or support of the victim may also request access to the recording in order to understand the sequence of events or way in which events unfolded. The CPS will also watch the recording in order to hear what the victim has said and how they said it. They will also be able to assess the witness's ability to answer questions and gain an insight in to how the victim will stand up to cross-examination. The victim themselves will also need to be shown the recording at some point prior to their giving evidence so that they can refresh their memories about the incident.

13.3.2 **Editing recordings**

Prior to any criminal proceedings at court, the defence or prosecution team involved in the proceedings can ask for the visual recording of the witness interview to be edited. This will be the subject of a court hearing when both the prosecution and defence teams will make representations to the court, who will in turn agree or disagree the content of any edits. The trial judge will always have the final say in these matters.

From a police perspective, there are several factors that will need to be taken into consideration when deciding who will complete the editing process. Firstly, the person who undertakes the editing process will need to prepare and sign an evidential statement. They will also be required to produce a new master tape of the interview which will require exhibiting, and they may futhermore be required to give sworn evidence at court about the process that they have undertaken. Secondly, this is work that is likely to require completion outside of normal working hours.

Example—Potential solution to urgent directions for video-editing

This example proffers a solution to situations in which a court directs that a video recording be edited within a few hours.

An officer is at court on the first day of the trial and the defence make an application to get the interview edited. The court decide for whatever reason that this application should be granted, and the trial is adjourned until 10.30am the next day so that the recording can be edited ready for court the following day. Who will complete this task? It is unlikely that an outside agency will drop everything just to edit one interview, and there is also the matter of confidentiality and security.

It may, therefore, be appropriate to nominate trained police officers, rather than civil staff for this task.

13.4 **Retention and Disposal of Recordings**

The retention and disposal of visually recorded statements will always be the subject of local policy. However, it would make sense that recordings should be retained in the case of a child witnesses until 7 years after the date of their 18th birthday; and in the case of a vulnerable adult witness, until 7 years after the date of completion of any criminal proceedings.

Once the officer in charge has collected all the interview recordings at the end of the proceedings, the master tapes can be sent for storage at a secure central storage location, and the working copies can be sent for destruction. Again, there will be local policies that will govern the way in which working copies of recordings will be disposed of.

13.5 **Digital or Analogue Recording Systems?**

Digital Versatile Disc (DVD) recordings will give a far superior visual quality than Video Home System (VHS) recordings and the audio quality is better than Compact Disk (CD) sound recordings. Most modern DVD recordings have a longevity of about 100 years.

DVD is also a non-deteriorating storage medium. This means that the quality of the recording will be exactly the same each time that it is played. It should, however, be remembered that DVDs can be damaged, so are not indestructible, and therefore should be handled with care. Although it is not immediately obvious, DVDs can bend, causing the disc to malfunction during playback; in some instances not playback at all.

However, if discs are stored appropriately in the correct type of storage box, they should be fine. While DVD technology is tolerant to minor scratches and fingerprint marks on the recorded surface, these should be avoided wherever possible. The careful handling and storage of DVD discs will ensure that the quality of recordings and their lifetime is maximized.

POINT TO NOTE—TIPS ON HANDLING AND STORAGE:

- Always handle DVDs by the outer edge or the centre hole;
- Use a non-solvent based felt-tip permanent marker to write on DVDs;
- Leave DVDs in their case when they are not being used;
- Remove dirt, fingerprints smudges, and liquids by wiping with a clean cotton cloth in a straight line from the centre of the DVD toward the outer edge.

13.6 Chapter Summary

Any visually recorded statement that is conducted with a vulnerable adult or child witness, prepared under the auspices of ABE in criminal proceedings and in compliance with the Youth Justice and Criminal Evidence Act 1999 will by its very nature be an emotive and extremely powerful piece of evidence in any criminal investigation and subsequent court proceedings.

Investigators should not lose sight of the fact that the recording is a visual and audio record of what could be some of the most sensitive and personal information that the witness has ever told anyone.

It is therefore desirable that any such recording with a vulnerable adult or child witness should be treated with the utmost care and its integrity and confidentially maintained at all times.

SPACE FOR NOTES

SPACE FOR NOTES

SPACE FOR NOTES

Ongoing Protection Orders

14.1 **Introduction**

Numerous orders are available for the initial and ongoing protection of children. These orders are issued by a family court as the result of a child coming to the notice of a local authority, usually in the form of child care proceedings. The legislation catering for these orders can be found in the Children Act 1989.

A family court can grant a range of orders that are issued to protect the rights of children and to ensure that the appropriate legal framework is put into place. There are also several initiatives and pieces of legislation that deal with the matters relating to the ongoing protection of victims of crime from intimidation or harassment.

14.2 **The Children Act 1989: Care Orders**

The Children Act 1989 is intended to protect children more effectively. If the social services believe that a child may be at risk or fear that they may be harmed, they can apply to the court for a care order under the Children Act 1989 in order to protect that child. Care proceedings are instigated in the Family Proceedings Court, and are regulated under guidelines known as the Protocol for Judicial Case Management in Public Law Children Act Cases. The guidelines state that any care proceedings should be finished within a maximum of 40 weeks of the application of an order, unless the case is complex or very complicated.

Care orders are usually taken by a local authority in relation to children who they believe are suffering or are likely to suffer significant harm in circumstances where:

- The harm is attributable to the care given to the child not being what it would be reasonable to expect a parent to give him or her; or
- The child is beyond parental control.

Care orders can remain in force until the child is 18 years old, unless the order is discharged by the court earlier. Orders may only be obtained in relation to children who are under 17 years of age (or under 16 if the child is married). The local authority will also have the responsibility to make sure that any plans that are made and any preparations started before the child reaches the age of 18 are implemented. This will enable the child to make the transition from being cared for into independence in the least traumatic way.

Following any application to the court, there will normally be a series of interim care orders under s 38 of the Children Act 1989 while further investigations and assessments are carried out before any final orders are made by the court.

Under s 33(3) of the Children Act 1989, while any care order is in existence, the local authority shall by virtue of the order have:

- Parental responsibility for the child;
- The power to determine the extent to which a parent or guardian of the child may meet his or her parental responsibility for him or her and empower them to make such decisions as:
  - Where the child will live;
  - With whom they will live; and
  - How the child will have contact with named persons.

Even though the local authority has parental responsibility, it cannot:

- Agree that the child can be adopted;
- Cause the child to be raised in a religion other than the one he or she would normally have been raised in if there had been no care order;
- Allow the child to reside anywhere outside of the UK for a period of more than 28 days without the consent of everyone who has parental responsibility, or a court order to that effect.

Once a care order has been issued, the child should be the subject of regular reviews to ensure that the child's needs are being met.

Any decision about an application for a care order will not be made at the first court hearing. The court can make several types of interim order at this hearing.

14.2.1 Interim Care Order

The court can make an Interim Care Order only if it decides there are good reasons to believe that the child has been seriously harmed or is likely to be seriously harmed. This order can last for up to eight weeks, and can be renewed for periods of four weeks after the expiry date. When this type of order is issued, the local authority will have shared parental responsibility with the parents. This will also include having the ultimate decision about where the child will live.

14.2.2 Interim Supervision Order

An Interim Supervision Order does not give parental responsibility, however, it does mean that the local authority will monitor how a child is being cared for.

14.2.3 Interim Residence Order

The court can make an Interim Residence Order if it is satisfied that a family member can care for the child until the final court hearing. The appointed person will then have shared parental responsibility for the child.

14.2.4 Interim Contact Order

If a child is living away from his or her parents, the court must have regard for what if any arrangements have been made or are proposed for the child to see his or her family. If the court is not satisfied or there are disagreements, then it can make a contact order setting out what the arrangements for contact should be.

14.2.5 **Residence Order**

A Residence Order will be issued when the court is satisfied that it needs to make decisions about where a child will live. Parents can make an application for a 'Joint Residence Order'; the courts are not keen on such orders as it will mean that the child will have to split his or her time between parents and this could lead to a disrupted upbringing. If a residence order is granted, the recipient of the order can only take the child who is the subject of the order out of the country for periods of less than one month at a time. Any deviation from this or an application to live out of the country must be approved by the court.

14.2.6 **Contact Order**

A Contact Order will deal with issues such as short visits with the parent who is not the holder of the residence order, including weekends and part of the holidays. A Contact Order can also set out where the contact visits should take place and at what time.

14.2.7 **Prohibited Steps Order**

An application may be made for this order to prevent one parent from doing something in relation to a child to which the other parent is opposed.

Example—Potential use of a Prohibited Steps Order: Removal of a child from the UK

If there are concerns that a parent is going to take a child out of the country against the wishes of the other parent they can apply for a 'Prohibited Steps Order'. If the child is subsequently removed from the country, the court can in certain circumstances assist in helping to get the child back, but this will depend on the country to which the child has been taken.

14.2.8 **Search and Find and Disclosure Orders**

An application can be made for a 'Search and Find Order' to return a child to his or her home address. The court can enlist the help of the police to make inquiries about the location of a child, or make an order for the police or an official acting on behalf of the court to enter and search an address where the child is located, and use such force as is necessary to retrieve that child.

14.2.9 Specific Issue Order

This is similar to a Prohibitive Steps Order, but is designed to deal with more day-to-day issues, such as which school a child should attend, if a child should have any particular medical treatment, or any other issues to do with the children on which the parents disagree.

14.3 Child Assessment Orders

A court can issue an order that will require a child to undergo an assessment (eg psychological or educational) to decide if a child is suffering 'significant harm'. The court will then decide, based on the assessment, whether it is appropriate to issue a care order. An assessment must not be for more than seven days.

14.4 No Order Principle

The Children Act 1989 was designed to deal with genuine disputes between parents and the local authority in order to safeguard the welfare of children. Therefore, minor matters that can be dealt with by agreement should not be referred to the court.

14.5 Wardship

The High Court has powers to make certain orders regarding children where they have been removed and are in serious danger or at risk. The court will make the child a ward of the court.

This means that the High Court will have responsibility for that child and no orders can be made or action taken which affect the child, unless permission is obtained from the High Court first.

14.6 Chapter Summary

This chapter has considered the issues associated with ongoing protection orders in respect of children. The 'no order' principle has been highlighted alongside a number of orders that are available under the Children Act 1989. The implications of wardship in the high court have also been discussed.

SPACE FOR NOTES

SPACE FOR NOTES

SPACE FOR NOTES

Witness Intimidation

15.1 **Introduction**

> Witnesses are essential to the success of the entire criminal justice system and the government is committed to providing better services and support to both victims and witnesses, to ensure that they see justice done more often and more quickly.
>
> Lord Falconer

Many victims opt out of the criminal justice process prior to the case ever getting to court because they are in fear or are intimidated. It is, therefore, vital that the agencies involved in this process work together to support each witness and understand the nature of the problem in order that they can offer the best advice and service to victims of crime.

Intimidation can manifest itself in many different ways; it can either be a physical threat to a person or to that person or another's property. It may take the form of written words or abusive behaviour, or simply the presence of another person near a victim may be enough to make them feel threatened. It should be remembered that intimidation is a personal thing and what would intimidate one person might not intimidate another.

It is important to establish the basis on which a witness feels intimidated and to address it as early as possible. In some instances, this may be achieved by explaining the role that the witness has to play in the court proceedings more fully than is often the case, in other instances special measures may be required, while in some cases some form of preventative measures might need to be taken up to and including witness protection.

15.2 **Witness Intimidation**

Witness intimidation is a criminal offence as follows:

> It is a criminal offence if a person knowingly performs an act intended to intimidate another person who is or may be a witness in civil or criminal proceedings (s 39 of the Criminal Justice and Police Act 2001).

In addition to this, intimidating a witness while the court is sitting is likely to amount to contempt (eg under s 12 of the Contempt of Court Act 1981 or s 118 of the County Courts Act 1984).

Rather than taking legal action against a person who intimidates a witness *after* the event, it may be possible to reduce the possibility of intimidation occurring in the first instance by the imposition of appropriate bail conditions on the defendant intended to prohibit contact with the witness. Such bail conditions typically include not contacting the witness and not going to the area in which the witness lives, works, or otherwise frequents.

15.3 **Witness Protection**

There are essentially two types of witness protection mechanism: those in which the anonymity of the witness is preserved during the criminal proceedings itself, and those in which the witness is re-located and given a new identity after the proceedings have taken place.

The first involves maintaining the anonymity of the witness during the trial itself. This can be facilitated by either the witness giving their evidence and having their cross-examination by live video link and by having the sound of their voice distorted to hide their identity, or by the victim or witness's evidence being given in private to a judge or prosecutor prior to the trial. Concealing the identity of a witness does, however, tend to fly in the face of the main principle of the British judicial system, which is that of an open justice system where the accused is able to face his or her accusers and test the evidence against them. Unless special exceptions apply, British courts are normally heard in public. However, the court has the power to withhold names and addresses of witnesses if it considers that it is appropriate to do so. In certain cases the court can make a decision that to disclose the identity of a victim or witness to anyone involved in the proceedings would seriously jeopardize their safety or wellbeing; accordingly the identity of that person or persons can be withheld from the proceedings. These occasions are likely to be rare and are a matter for the discretion of the judge: *R v Taylor (G)*, TLR 17 August 1994. Embarrassment by a witness will not constitute sufficient grounds for seeking anonymity, *R v Malvern JJ, ex p Evans* [1988] QB 553.

The second usually only covers the period after the criminal proceedings have taken place. In this instance, the victim or witness gives their evidence in the normal way, with such steps as may be necessary being taken in court to reduce the possibility any form of intimidation during the proceedings. After the proceedings, a variety of measures might be put into place for the ongoing protection of the witness, including being moved to a new geographical area and being given a new identity, although such measures tend to be reserved for more extreme cases of intimidation because of the cost and long-term commitment involved. In a small number of cases, often those involving national security, it may be that a witness is moved to a new geographical area and given a new identity while the case is waiting to go to trial. In these instances, the steps taken to protect the witness would need to be reviewed after the trial.

15.4 **The Multi-Agency Witness Mobility Scheme**

The multi-agency witness mobility scheme was brought about to help the police and local authorities to move intimidated witnesses in an organized, and supported fashion.

On occasions when it is judged that there is a serious risk to the victim or witness, then they will be offered the chance to move quickly from the dangerous environment in which they find themselves to a similar environment somewhere else where they will be safe.

15.5 **Chapter Summary**

No matter how well an investigation is conducted, without witnesses investigators will often not have enough evidence to proceed with a criminal investigation. Why is it then that while investigators and other professionals acknowledge that the witness plays a vital part in any investigation, they are often treated with indifference and once a statement has been obtained left to their own devices and, despite promises of support and protection, simply left to get on with things for themselves?

By spending a little more time ensuring that witnesses are made to feel cared for and safe throughout the whole process from first contact to the point after they have given their evidence and the trial has been completed, more witnesses are likely to come forward and support criminal prosecutions.

There are now increasing changes in guidance and initiatives designed to support witnesses and increase witness care, but without someone to implement such initiatives witnesses will not be able to reap the benefits.

SPACE FOR NOTES

SPACE FOR NOTES

16

Pre-Trial Therapy

16.1 **Introduction**

Counselling and therapy can help a victim understand that they are not to blame and it can help them to cope with the devastating feelings of guilt and shame that some victims experience. A victim who initially appears to be coping with their ordeal may not have properly come to terms with what has happened or may even be in denial. Victims will sometimes only disclose a small part of the story about the abuse until they feel safe and secure enough to disclose the whole story. It is at such times that they may need counselling or therapy to help them come to terms with what has happened and to cope with their feelings.

Consideration should always be given to a victim's welfare and therapeutic needs, and be carefully balanced against the possible impact that therapy might have on a criminal trial and the consequences for the victim.

16.2 **Pre-Interview Therapy**

Therapy has never been encouraged before a visually recorded statement has taken place since lawyers have always argued that any form of therapy may have an adverse affect on the victim's evidence. This situation clearly raises the possibility of a prosecution being seriously jeopardized.

16.3 **Pre-Trial Therapy**

There are two broad categories of therapy that can take place before a criminal trial starts, counselling and psychotherapy.

POINT TO NOTE—COUNSELLING

Counselling covers three main topic areas:

- The impact of the abuse on the victim;
- The overall well-being of the victim.
- Imparting information on matters such as trust and abusive relationships.

POINT TO NOTE—PSYCHOTHERAPY

Psychotherapy covers two main topic areas:

- The treatment of matters such as post-traumatic stress disorder (PTSD) or other behavioural conditions;
- Issues surrounding the broader matter of a victim's mental health connected to a traumatic incident.

Any form of therapy could require the long-term involvement of a therapist, this will be dependent on the victim themselves and the incident that they have been involved in.

Victims and witnesses may derive therapeutic value from simply talking to someone about the incident under investigation. Such conversation could, therefore, be described as therapy. Any conversation, however, between witnesses that occurs before a criminal trial starts could be open to challenge from the defence on the basis that it gives rise to the possibility of witnesses giving unreliable or inconsistent accounts while giving evidence or giving false evidence either deliberately or accidentally.

Prior to any criminal proceedings, group therapy where the victim is asked to specifically recount the incident or specifics of the alleged abuse should, wherever possible, be avoided due to the implications that this may have for a criminal prosecution.

Example—Witnesses and group therapy

For example, a witness in group therapy may:

Overhear an account of the same incident that they have observed, and fill in gaps or omissions in their own account with information from another witness who observed the incident from a different prospective. The additional information is evidence that the witness couldn't possibly have seen or heard from where they were observing the incident.

Or

Not consciously listen to or overhear a similar account of the same incident but with additional information included, and not realizing that they have retained this additional information, therefore not knowing its origins or how or where to credit it, own the information themselves as information that they have themselves observed.

When asked, therefore, to disclose what they have seen they may disclose information that is not wholly their own. The second example may include information from Radio, TV, or newspapers as a result of conversation with unconnected parties who have not witnessed the incident themselves but have read or heard about it in the media.

All notes and associated material that is produced as a result of the counselling process must be saved and preserved in its original format in the event that the notes are required for disclosure purposes in criminal proceedings. The issue of how relevant such information may be to the proceedings will be for the CPS to decide.

Guarantees about the confidentiality of counsellors' notes cannot be made to victims or witnesses in advance, it is therefore imperative that an understanding is reached with the victim or witness at the outset of therapy.

16.4 **Pre-Court Preparation**

It is considered acceptable to undertake a course of action to prepare a witness or victim for their appearance in court prior to any criminal proceedings taking place. The purpose of this work is to:

- Give the victim or witness relevant information about the criminal justice system and of the processes involved;
- Confront any fears or concerns which the victim may hold in relation to the proceedings and about the mechanics of the evidence giving process itself;
- To reduce any anxieties that the victim or witness may have.

16.4.1 **Timing of any preparation**

The effective administration and timing of any pre-court preparation for a victim or witness is vital. If it is introduced too soon any concerns or worries may be exacerbated, on the other hand, if it is left until immediately before the commencement of the proceedings, the victim or witness may feel that they are being rushed, and therefore not have adequate time to consider all the implications of the information that they have given.

16.5 **Chapter Summary**

Whether a victim or witness should receive any form of therapy prior to the start of criminal proceedings is not a decision that should be made by the police or the CPS alone. These types of decisions should only be made at a multi-agency strategy meeting with those who are responsible for the welfare of the victim or witness, in consultation with the victim's or witness's primary carers and the victim or witness themselves.

If the CPS advises that any form of therapy may prejudice the criminal proceedings, those responsible for the victim's wellbeing should consider this when they make any decisions about the provision of therapy. Despite the fact that the provision of therapy may prejudice the criminal proceedings it may still be in the best interests of the victim or witness to provide them with the therapy.

If therapy is to be provided it should be one-to-one and the therapist advised about the possible consequences of the counselling and advice given about the recording of notes.

During therapeutic sessions, victims or witnesses should never be encouraged to expand on the account that they have already given to the police. Any new disclosures or new lines of investigation that are made by the victim or witness, or any inconsistency with the initial disclosure should be reported to the police.

Some therapies should be avoided at all costs, as they would most definitely cause problems where a criminal prosecution is concerned. Such therapies include regression techniques, hypnosis, and psychodrama.

SPACE FOR NOTES

SPACE FOR NOTES

SPACE FOR NOTES

SPACE FOR NOTES

What's on the Horizon?

17.1 **Introduction**

At the time of writing, two pieces of legislation that will have an impact on investigations involving vulnerable witnesses were awaiting implementation:

- Section 137 of the Criminal Justice Act 2003; and
- The Mental Capacity Act 2005.

17.2 **Section 137 of the Criminal Justice Act 2003**

Witnesses for the purposes of s 137 of the Criminal Justice Act 2003 (CJA) are those who have or claim to have witnessed, visually or otherwise:

- An offence;
- Part of an offence; or
- Events closely connected with an offence (including the acquisition or disposal of anything involved in the offence and any incriminating comments made by an alleged offender either before or after the offence).

An offence for the purposes of s 137 can either:

- Only be tried at the Crown Court on indictment; or
- Be tried either at the Magistrates' or Crown Court provided it has been designated as coming within the scope of this piece of legislation by the Home Secretary.

Video recordings of interviews with these witnesses can be admitted as evidence-in-chief if their recollection of the events is likely to be significantly better at the time of the interview than at the time of giving evidence. Courts will take account of the length of the interval between the alleged event and the interview when considering this question.

The criterion for the admission of video-recorded interviews as evidence-in-chief is, therefore, different than it is under the Youth Justice and Criminal Evidence Act 1999 (YJCEA). In the case of the CJA, the criterion amounts to one of the events being fresh in the witness's memory at the time of the interview. In the case of the YJCEA, the criterion is one of maximizing the quality of a witness's evidence that would otherwise be limited by virtue of an inherent or a situational vulnerability. In these circumstances, it may be that in some situations an application to play a video-recorded interview with a vulnerable witness as evidence-in-chief is more likely to be successful if made under the CJA than if made under the YJCEA.

The information available at the time of writing suggests that s 137 of the CJA is due to be implemented in 2008 or 2009.

17.3 **The Mental Capacity Act 2005**

Sections 1 to 8 of Part I of the Mental Capacity Act 2005 (MCA) are reproduced in Appendix B for reference.

The MCA applies to anyone over 16 who lacks mental capacity and where a 'decision' needs to be made. A 'decision' covers a wide range of matters and would include consent for a video-recorded interview and a medical examination. The Act establishes the principle that everybody should be assumed to have capacity unless established otherwise. It goes on to point out that a communication issue should not be confused with a capacity issue in that every effort should be made to communicate with people, using whatever methods are necessary. An intermediary may be of use in these circumstances (see point 11.11.2 above).

If following an assessment (the extent of the 'assessment' depends on the circumstances), it is concluded that lack of capacity is an issue, actions should be taken in the 'best interests' of the witness. As far as possible, when considering the witness's 'best interests' particular account should be taken of:

- The witness's past and present wishes and feelings;
- The beliefs and values that would be likely to influence the witness's decision if they had capacity; and
- Other factors that the witness would be likely to consider if they were able to do so.

When trying to establish these matters, particular account should be taken of the following views:

- Such views as the witness is able to express (with such assistance as is necessary); and
- Where it is practicable and appropriate to consult them, the views of:
  - Anyone named by the witness as someone to be consulted on the matter in question or on matters of that kind;
  - Anyone engaged in caring for the witness or interested in their welfare;
  - Any person with lasting power of attorney granted by the witness; and
  - Any deputy appointed for the witness by a court.

Where somebody who is involved in the care of a person believed to lack capacity is also suspected of abusing them, this should be taken into account when considering their views on the witness's best interests.

The scope of the consultation with others involved in the care, welfare, and treatment of the witness lacking capacity very much depends on the nature of the decision and the time available in the circumstances—this means taking account of the urgency of the case and the time at which it arises.

When considering best interests, account should also be taken of any possibility that the witness will regain capacity and if so when this is likely to be (s 4[3] of the MCA). This is important in circumstances where, for example, the effect of a witness's medication on their capacity to make a decision changes over time or when a witness is likely to recover from an injury or an illness to the extent that they are likely to be able more fully to participate in the process of making a decision.

The information available at the time of writing suggests that the Mental Capacity Act 2005 will be implemented in phases commencing 1 April 2007.

17.4 **Chapter Summary**

This chapter has attempted to highlight those pieces of legislation that are likely to have an impact on investigations involving vulnerable witnesses when they are implemented.

Briefly, section 137 of the Criminal Justice Act 2003 provides alternative grounds for making an application to admit the video recording of an interview with any witness, including a vulnerable witness, as evidence-in-chief. The Mental Capacity Act 2005 has implications for the decision-making of vulnerable witnesses.

SPACE FOR NOTES

SPACE FOR NOTES

SPACE FOR NOTES

Appendix A

Youth Justice and Criminal Evidence Act 1999 PART II, Chapters I to V

CHAPTER I

SPECIAL MEASURES DIRECTIONS IN CASE OF VULNERABLE
AND INTIMIDATED WITNESSES

Preliminary

16. Witnesses eligible for assistance on grounds of age or incapacity

(1) For the purposes of this Chapter a witness in criminal proceedings (other than the accused) is eligible for assistance by virtue of this section—
  (a) if under the age of 17 at the time of the hearing; or
  (b) if the court considers that the quality of evidence given by the witness is likely to be diminished by reason of any circumstances falling within subsection (2).

(2) The circumstances falling within this subsection are—
  (a) that the witness—
    (i) suffers from mental disorder within the meaning of the Mental Health Act 1983, or
    (ii) otherwise has a significant impairment of intelligence and social functioning;
  (b) that the witness has a physical disability or is suffering from a physical disorder.

(3) In subsection (1)(a) 'the time of the hearing', in relation to a witness, means the time when it falls to the court to make a determination for the purposes of section 19(2) in relation to the witness.

(4) In determining whether a witness falls within subsection (1)(b) the court must consider any views expressed by the witness.

(5) In this Chapter references to the quality of a witness's evidence are to its quality in terms of completeness, coherence and accuracy; and for this purpose 'coherence' refers to a witness's ability in giving evidence to give answers which address the questions put to the witness and can be understood both individually and collectively.

17. Witnesses eligible for assistance on grounds of fear or distress about testifying

(1) For the purposes of this Chapter a witness in criminal proceedings (other than the accused) is eligible for assistance by virtue of this subsection if the court is satisfied that the quality of evidence given by the witness is likely to be diminished

by reason of fear or distress on the part of the witness in connection with testifying in the proceedings.

(2) In determining whether a witness falls within subsection (1) the court must take into account, in particular—

    (a) the nature and alleged circumstances of the offence to which the proceedings relate;

    (b) the age of the witness;

    (c) such of the following matters as appear to the court to be relevant, namely—

        (i) the social and cultural background and ethnic origins of the witness,

        (ii) the domestic and employment circumstances of the witness, and

        (iii) any religious beliefs or political opinions of the witness;

    (d) any behaviour towards the witness on the part of—

        (i) the accused,

        (ii) members of the family or associates of the accused, or

        (iii) any other person who is likely to be an accused or a witness in the proceedings.

(3) In determining that question the court must in addition consider any views expressed by the witness.

(4) Where the complainant in respect of a sexual offence is a witness in proceedings relating to that offence (or to that offence and any other offences), the witness is eligible for assistance in relation to those proceedings by virtue of this subsection unless the witness has informed the court of the witness's wish not to be so eligible by virtue of this subsection.

18. Special measures available to eligible witnesses

(1) For the purposes of this Chapter—

    (a) the provision which may be made by a special measures direction by virtue of each of sections 23 to 30 is a special measure available in relation to a witness eligible for assistance by virtue of section 16; and

    (b) the provision which may be made by such a direction by virtue of each of sections 23 to 28 is a special measure available in relation to a witness eligible for assistance by virtue of section 17;

but this subsection has effect subject to subsection (2).

(2) Where (apart from this subsection) a special measure would, in accordance with subsection (1)(a) or (b), be available in relation to a witness in any proceedings, it shall not be taken by a court to be available in relation to the witness unless—

    (a) the court has been notified by the Secretary of State that relevant arrangements may be made available in the area in which it appears to the court that the proceedings will take place, and

    (b) the notice has not been withdrawn.

(3) In subsection (2) 'relevant arrangements' means arrangements for implementing the measure in question which cover the witness and the proceedings in question.

(4) The withdrawal of a notice under that subsection relating to a special measure shall not affect the availability of that measure in relation to a witness if a special measures direction providing for that measure to apply to the witness's evidence has been made by the court before the notice is withdrawn.

(5) The Secretary of State may by order make such amendments of this Chapter as he considers appropriate for altering the special measures which, in accordance with subsection (1)(a) or (b), are available in relation to a witness eligible for assistance by virtue of section 16 or (as the case may be) section 17, whether—

    (a) by modifying the provisions relating to any measure for the time being available in relation to such a witness,

    (b) by the addition—

        (i) (with or without modifications) of any measure which is for the time being available in relation to a witness eligible for assistance by virtue of the other of those sections, or

        (ii) of any new measure, or

    (c) by the removal of any measure.

19. Special measures direction relating to eligible witness

(1) This section applies where in any criminal proceedings—

    (a) a party to the proceedings makes an application for the court to give a direction under this section in relation to a witness in the proceedings other than the accused, or

    (b) the court of its own motion raises the issue whether such a direction should be given.

(2) Where the court determines that the witness is eligible for assistance by virtue of section 16 or 17, the court must then—

    (a) determine whether any of the special measures available in relation to the witness (or any combination of them) would, in its opinion, be likely to improve the quality of evidence given by the witness; and

    (b) if so—

        (i) determine which of those measures (or combination of them) would, in its opinion, be likely to maximise so far as practicable the quality of such evidence; and

        (ii) give a direction under this section providing for the measure or measures so determined to apply to evidence given by the witness.

(3) In determining for the purposes of this Chapter whether any special measure or measures would or would not be likely to improve, or to maximise so far as practicable, the quality of evidence given by the witness, the court must consider all the circumstances of the case, including in particular—

    (a) any views expressed by the witness; and

    (b) whether the measure or measures might tend to inhibit such evidence being effectively tested by a party to the proceedings.

(4) A special measures direction must specify particulars of the provision made by the direction in respect of each special measure which is to apply to the witness's evidence.

(5) In this Chapter 'special measures direction' means a direction under this section.

(6) Nothing in this Chapter is to be regarded as affecting any power of a court to make an order or give leave of any description (in the exercise of its inherent jurisdiction or otherwise)—

    (a) in relation to a witness who is not an eligible witness, or

    (b) in relation to an eligible witness where (as, for example, in a case where a foreign language interpreter is to be provided) the order is made or the leave is given otherwise than by reason of the fact that the witness is an eligible witness.

20. Further provisions about directions: general

(1) Subject to subsection (2) and section 21(8), a special measures direction has binding effect from the time it is made until the proceedings for the purposes of which it is made are either—

    (a) determined (by acquittal, conviction or otherwise), or

    (b) abandoned,

in relation to the accused or (if there is more than one) in relation to each of the accused.

(2) The court may discharge or vary (or further vary) a special measures direction if it appears to the court to be in the interests of justice to do so, and may do so either—

    (a) on an application made by a party to the proceedings, if there has been a material change of circumstances since the relevant time, or

    (b) of its own motion.

(3) In subsection (2) 'the relevant time' means—

    (a) the time when the direction was given, or

    (b) if a previous application has been made under that subsection, the time when the application (or last application) was made.

(4) Nothing in section 24(2) and (3), 27(4) to (7) or 28(4) to (6) is to be regarded as affecting the power of the court to vary or discharge a special measures direction under subsection (2)

(5) The court must state in open court its reasons for—

    (a) giving or varying,

    (b) refusing an application for, or for the variation or discharge of, or

    (c) discharging,

a special measures direction and, if it is a magistrates' court, must cause them to be entered in the register of its proceedings

(6) Rules of court may make provision—

    (a) for uncontested applications to be determined by the court without a hearing;

    (b) for preventing the renewal of an unsuccessful application for a special measures direction except where there has been a material change of circumstances;

    (c) for expert evidence to be given in connection with an application for, or for varying or discharging, such a direction;

    (d) for the manner in which confidential or sensitive information is to be treated in connection with such an application and in particular as to its being disclosed to, or withheld from, a party to the proceedings.

21. Special provisions relating to child witnesses

(1) For the purposes of this section—

    (a) a witness in criminal proceedings is a 'child witness' if he is an eligible witness by reason of section 16(1)(a) (whether or not he is an eligible witness by reason of any other provision of section 16 or 17);

    (b) a child witness is 'in need of special protection' if the offence (or any of the offences) to which the proceedings relate is—

        (i) an offence falling within section 35(3)(a) (sexual offences etc.), or

        (ii) an offence falling within section 35(3)(b), (c) or (d) (kidnapping, assaults etc.); and

    (c) a 'relevant recording', in relation to a child witness, is a video recording of an interview of the witness made with a view to its admission as evidence in chief of the witness.

(2) Where the court, in making a determination for the purposes of section 19(2), determines that a witness in criminal proceedings is a child witness, the court must—

    (a) first have regard to subsections (3) to (7) below; and

    (b) then have regard to section 19(2);

and for the purposes of section 19(2), as it then applies to the witness, any special measures required to be applied in relation to him by virtue of this section shall be treated as if they were measures determined by the court, pursuant to section 19(2)(a) and (b)(i), to be ones that (whether on their own or with any other special measures) would be likely to maximise, so far as practicable, the quality of his evidence.

(3) The primary rule in the case of a child witness is that the court must give a special measures direction in relation to the witness which complies with the following requirements—

    (a) it must provide for any relevant recording to be admitted under section 27 (video recorded evidence in chief); and

    (b) it must provide for any evidence given by the witness in the proceedings which is not given by means of a video recording (whether in chief or otherwise) to be given by means of a live link in accordance with section 24.

(4) The primary rule is subject to the following limitations—

    (a) the requirement contained in subsection (3)(a) or (b) has effect subject to the availability (within the meaning of section 18(2)) of the special measure in question in relation to the witness;

    (b) the requirement contained in subsection (3)(a) also has effect subject to section 27(2); and

    (c) the rule does not apply to the extent that the court is satisfied that compliance with it would not be likely to maximise the quality of the witness's evidence so far as practicable (whether because the application to that evidence of one or more other special measures available in relation to the witness would have that result or for any other reason).

(5) However, subsection (4)(c) does not apply in relation to a child witness in need of special protection.

(6) Where a child witness is in need of special protection by virtue of subsection (1)(b)(i), any special measures direction given by the court which complies with the requirement contained in subsection (3)(a) must in addition provide for the special measure available under section 28 (video recorded cross-examination or re-examination) to apply in relation to—

    (a) any cross-examination of the witness otherwise than by the accused in person, and

    (b) any subsequent re-examination.

(7) The requirement contained in subsection (6) has effect subject to the following limitations—

    (a) it has effect subject to the availability (within the meaning of section 18(2)) of that special measure in relation to the witness; and

    (b) it does not apply if the witness has informed the court that he does not want that special measure to apply in relation to him.

(8) Where a special measures direction is given in relation to a child witness who is an eligible witness by reason only of section 16(1)(a), then—

    (a) subject to subsection (9) below, and

    (b) except where the witness has already begun to give evidence in the proceedings,

the direction shall cease to have effect at the time when the witness attains the age of 17.

(9) Where a special measures direction is given in relation to a child witness who is an eligible witness by reason only of section 16(1)(a) and—

    (a) the direction provides—

        (i) for any relevant recording to be admitted under section 27 as evidence in chief of the witness, or

        (ii) for the special measure available under section 28 to apply in relation to the witness, and

    (b) if it provides for that special measure to so apply, the witness is still under the age of 17 when the video recording is made for the purposes of section 28,

then, so far as it provides as mentioned in paragraph (a)(i) or (ii) above, the direction shall continue to have effect in accordance with section 20(1) even though the witness subsequently attains that age.

22. Extension of provisions of section 21 to certain witnesses over 17

(1) For the purposes of this section—

    (a) a witness in criminal proceedings (other than the accused) is a 'qualifying witness' if he—

        (i) is not an eligible witness at the time of the hearing (as defined by section 16(3)), but

        (ii) was under the age of 17 when a relevant recording was made;

    (b) a qualifying witness is 'in need of special protection' if the offence (or any of the offences) to which the proceedings relate is—

        (i) an offence falling within section 35(3)(a) (sexual offences etc.), or

        (ii) an offence falling within section 35(3)(b), (c) or (d) (kidnapping, assaults etc.); and

    (c) a 'relevant recording', in relation to a witness, is a video recording of an interview of the witness made with a view to its admission as evidence in chief of the witness.

(2) Subsections (2) to (7) of section 21 shall apply as follows in relation to a qualifying witness—

    (a) subsections (2) to (4), so far as relating to the giving of a direction complying with the requirement contained in subsection (3)(a), shall apply to a qualifying witness in respect of the relevant recording as they apply to a child witness (within the meaning of that section);

(b) subsection (5), so far as relating to the giving of such a direction, shall apply to a qualifying witness in need of special protection as it applies to a child witness in need of special protection (within the meaning of that section); and

(c) subsections (6) and (7) shall apply to a qualifying witness in need of special protection by virtue of subsection (1)(b)(i) above as they apply to such a child witness as is mentioned in subsection (6)

Special Measures

23. Screening witness from accused

(1) A special measures direction may provide for the witness, while giving testimony or being sworn in court, to be prevented by means of a screen or other arrangement from seeing the accused.

(2) But the screen or other arrangement must not prevent the witness from being able to see, and to be seen by—

(a) the judge or justices (or both) and the jury (if there is one);

(b) legal representatives acting in the proceedings; and

(c) any interpreter or other person appointed (in pursuance of the direction or otherwise) to assist the witness.

(3) Where two or more legal representatives are acting for a party to the proceedings, subsection (2)(b) is to be regarded as satisfied in relation to those representatives if the witness is able at all material times to see and be seen by at least one of them.

24. Evidence by live link

(1) A special measures direction may provide for the witness to give evidence by means of a live link.

(2) Where a direction provides for the witness to give evidence by means of a live link, the witness may not give evidence in any other way without the permission of the court

(3) The court may give permission for the purposes of subsection (2) if it appears to the court to be in the interests of justice to do so, and may do so either—

(a) on an application by a party to the proceedings, if there has been a material change of circumstances since the relevant time, or

(b) of its own motion.

(4) In subsection (3) 'the relevant time' means—

(a) the time when the direction was given, or

(b) if a previous application has been made under that subsection, the time when the application (or last application) was made.

(5) Where in proceedings before a magistrates' court—

(a) evidence is to be given by means of a live link in accordance with a special measures direction, but

(b) suitable facilities for receiving such evidence are not available at any petty-sessional court-house in which that court can (apart from this subsection) lawfully sit, the court may sit for the purposes of the whole or any part of those proceedings at a place where such facilities are available and which has been appointed for the purposes of this subsection by the justices acting for the petty sessions area for which the court acts.

(6) A place appointed under subsection (5) may be outside the petty sessions area for which it is appointed; but (if so) it is to be regarded as being in that area for the purpose of the jurisdiction of the justices acting for that area.

(7) In this section 'petty-sessional court-house' has the same meaning as in the Magistrates' Courts Act 1980 and 'petty sessions area' has the same meaning as in the Justices of the Peace Act 1997.

(8) In this Chapter 'live link' means a live television link or other arrangement whereby a witness, while absent from the courtroom or other place where the proceedings are being held, is able to see and hear a person there and to be seen and heard by the persons specified in section 23(2)(a) to (c).

25. Evidence given in private.

(1) A special measures direction may provide for the exclusion from the court, during the giving of the witness's evidence, of persons of any description specified in the direction.

(2) The persons who may be so excluded do not include—
    (a) the accused,
    (b) legal representatives acting in the proceedings, or
    (c) any interpreter or other person appointed (in pursuance of the direction or otherwise) to assist the witness.

(3) A special measures direction providing for representatives of news gathering or reporting organisations to be so excluded shall be expressed not to apply to one named person who—
    (a) is a representative of such an organisation, and
    (b) has been nominated for the purpose by one or more such organisations,
unless it appears to the court that no such nomination has been made.

(4) A special measures direction may only provide for the exclusion of persons under this section where—
    (a) the proceedings relate to a sexual offence; or
    (b) it appears to the court that there are reasonable grounds for believing that any person other than the accused has sought, or will seek, to intimidate the witness in connection with testifying in the proceedings.

(5) Any proceedings from which persons are excluded under this section (whether or not those persons include representatives of news gathering or reporting organisations) shall nevertheless be taken to be held in public for the purposes of any privilege or exemption from liability available in respect of fair, accurate and contemporaneous reports of legal proceedings held in public.

26. Removal of wigs and gowns

A special measures direction may provide for the wearing of wigs or gowns to be dispensed with during the giving of the witness's evidence.

27. Video recorded evidence in chief

(1) A special measures direction may provide for a video recording of an interview of the witness to be admitted as evidence in chief of the witness.

(2) A special measures direction may, however, not provide for a video recording, or a part of such a recording, to be admitted under this section if the court is of the opinion, having regard to all the circumstances of the case, that in the interests of justice the recording, or that part of it, should not be so admitted.

(3) In considering for the purposes of subsection (2) whether any part of a recording should not be admitted under this section, the court must consider whether any prejudice to the accused which might result from that part being so admitted is outweighed by the desirability of showing the whole, or substantially the whole, of the recorded interview

(4) Where a special measures direction provides for a recording to be admitted under this section, the court may nevertheless subsequently direct that it is not to be so admitted if—

    (a) it appears to the court that—

        (i) the witness will not be available for cross-examination (whether conducted in the ordinary way or in accordance with any such direction), and

        (ii) the parties to the proceedings have not agreed that there is no need for the witness to be so available; or

    (b) any rules of court requiring disclosure of the circumstances in which the recording was made have not been complied with to the satisfaction of the court.

(5) Where a recording is admitted under this section—

    (a) the witness must be called by the party tendering it in evidence, unless—

        (i) a special measures direction provides for the witness's evidence on cross-examination to be given otherwise than by testimony in court, or

        (ii) the parties to the proceedings have agreed as mentioned in subsection (4)(a)(ii); and

    (b) the witness may not give evidence in chief otherwise than by means of the recording—

        (i) as to any matter which, in the opinion of the court, has been dealt with adequately in the witness's recorded testimony, or

        (ii) without the permission of the court, as to any other matter which, in the opinion of the court, is dealt with in that testimony.

(6) Where in accordance with subsection (2) a special measures direction provides for part only of a recording to be admitted under this section, references in subsections (4) and (5) to the recording or to the witness's recorded testimony are references to the part of the recording or testimony which is to be so admitted

(7) The court may give permission for the purposes of subsection (5)(b)(ii) if it appears to the court to be in the interests of justice to do so, and may do so either—

    (a) on an application by a party to the proceedings, if there has been a material change of circumstances since the relevant time, or

    (b) of its own motion.

(8) In subsection (7) 'the relevant time' means—
  (a) the time when the direction was given, or
  (b) if a previous application has been made under that subsection, the time when the application (or last application) was made.

(9) The court may, in giving permission for the purposes of subsection (5)(b)(ii), direct that the evidence in question is to be given by the witness by means of a live link; and, if the court so directs, subsections (5) to (7) of section 24 shall apply in relation to that evidence as they apply in relation to evidence which is to be given in accordance with a special measures direction.

(10) A magistrates' court inquiring into an offence as examining justices under section 6 of the Magistrates' Courts Act 1980 may consider any video recording in relation to which it is proposed to apply for a special measures direction providing for it to be admitted at the trial in accordance with this section.

(11) Nothing in this section affects the admissibility of any video recording which would be admissible apart from this section.

28. Video recorded cross-examination or re-examination

(1) Where a special measures direction provides for a video recording to be admitted under section 27 as evidence in chief of the witness, the direction may also provide—
  (a) for any cross-examination of the witness, and any re-examination, to be recorded by means of a video recording; and
  (b) for such a recording to be admitted, so far as it relates to any such cross-examination or re-examination, as evidence of the witness under cross-examination or on re-examination, as the case may be.

(2) Such a recording must be made in the presence of such persons as rules of court or the direction may provide and in the absence of the accused, but in circumstances in which—
  (a) the judge or justices (or both) and legal representatives acting in the proceedings are able to see and hear the examination of the witness and to communicate with the persons in whose presence the recording is being made, and
  (b) the accused is able to see and hear any such examination and to communicate with any legal representative acting for him.

(3) Where two or more legal representatives are acting for a party to the proceedings, subsection (2)(a) and (b) are to be regarded as satisfied in relation to those representatives if at all material times they are satisfied in relation to at least one of them.

(4) Where a special measures direction provides for a recording to be admitted under this section, the court may nevertheless subsequently direct that it is not to be so admitted if any requirement of subsection (2) or rules of court or the direction has not been complied with to the satisfaction of the court.

(5) Where in pursuance of subsection (1) a recording has been made of any examination of the witness, the witness may not be subsequently cross-examined or re-examined in respect of any evidence given by the witness in the proceedings (whether in any recording admissible under section 27 or this section or otherwise than in such a recording) unless the court gives a further special measures direction making such provision as is mentioned in subsection (1)(a) and (b) in

relation to any subsequent cross-examination, and re-examination, of the witness.

(6) The court may only give such a further direction if it appears to the court—

(a) that the proposed cross-examination is sought by a party to the proceedings as a result of that party having become aware, since the time when the original recording was made in pursuance of subsection (1), of a matter which that party could not with reasonable diligence have ascertained by then, or

(b) that for any other reason it is in the interests of justice to give the further direction.

(7) Nothing in this section shall be read as applying in relation to any cross-examination of the witness by the accused in person (in a case where the accused is to be able to conduct any such cross-examination).

29. Examination of witness through intermediary

(1) A special measures direction may provide for any examination of the witness (however and wherever conducted) to be conducted through an interpreter or other person approved by the court for the purposes of this section ('an intermediary').

(2) The function of an intermediary is to communicate—

(a) to the witness, questions put to the witness, and

(b) to any person asking such questions, the answers given by the witness in reply to them,

and to explain such questions or answers so far as necessary to enable them to be understood by the witness or person in question.

(3) Any examination of the witness in pursuance of subsection (1) must take place in the presence of such persons as rules of court or the direction may provide, but in circumstances in which—

(a) the judge or justices (or both) and legal representatives acting in the proceedings are able to see and hear the examination of the witness and to communicate with the intermediary, and

(b) (except in the case of a video recorded examination) the jury (if there is one) are able to see and hear the examination of the witness.

(4) Where two or more legal representatives are acting for a party to the proceedings, subsection (3)(a) is to be regarded as satisfied in relation to those representatives if at all material times it is satisfied in relation to at least one of them

(5) A person may not act as an intermediary in a particular case except after making a declaration, in such form as may be prescribed by rules of court, that he will faithfully perform his function as intermediary.

(6) Subsection (1) does not apply to an interview of the witness which is recorded by means of a video recording with a view to its admission as evidence in chief of the witness; but a special measures direction may provide for such a recording to be admitted under section 27 if the interview was conducted through an intermediary and—

(a) that person complied with subsection (5) before the interview began, and

(b) the court's approval for the purposes of this section is given before the direction is given.

(7) Section 1 of the Perjury Act 1911 (perjury) shall apply in relation to a person acting as an intermediary as it applies in relation to a person lawfully sworn as

an interpreter in a judicial proceeding; and for this purpose, where a person acts as an intermediary in any proceeding which is not a judicial proceeding for the purposes of that section, that proceeding shall be taken to be part of the judicial proceeding in which the witness's evidence is given.

30. Aids to communication

A special measures direction may provide for the witness, while giving evidence (whether by testimony in court or otherwise), to be provided with such device as the court considers appropriate with a view to enabling questions or answers to be communicated to or by the witness despite any disability or disorder or other impairment which the witness has or suffers from.

Supplementary

31. Status of evidence given under Chapter I

(1) Subsections (2) to (4) apply to a statement made by a witness in criminal proceedings which, in accordance with a special measures direction, is not made by the witness in direct oral testimony in court but forms part of the witness's evidence in those proceedings

(2) The statement shall be treated as if made by the witness in direct oral testimony in court; and accordingly—

   (a) it is admissible evidence of any fact of which such testimony from the witness would be admissible;

   (b) it is not capable of corroborating any other evidence given by the witness.

(3) Subsection (2) applies to a statement admitted under section 27 or 28 which is not made by the witness on oath even though it would have been required to be made on oath if made by the witness in direct oral testimony in court.

(4) In estimating the weight (if any) to be attached to the statement, the court must have regard to all the circumstances from which an inference can reasonably be drawn (as to the accuracy of the statement or otherwise)

(5) Nothing in this Chapter (apart from subsection (3)) affects the operation of any rule of law relating to evidence in criminal proceedings.

(6) Where any statement made by a person on oath in any proceeding which is not a judicial proceeding for the purposes of section 1 of the Perjury Act 1911 (perjury) is received in evidence in pursuance of a special measures direction, that proceeding shall be taken for the purposes of that section to be part of the judicial proceeding in which the statement is so received in evidence

(7) Where in any proceeding which is not a judicial proceeding for the purposes of that Act—

   (a) a person wilfully makes a false statement otherwise than on oath which is subsequently received in evidence in pursuance of a special measures direction, and

   (b) the statement is made in such circumstances that had it been given on oath in any such judicial proceeding that person would have been guilty of perjury,

he shall be guilty of an offence and liable to any punishment which might be imposed on conviction of an offence under section 57(2) (giving of false unsworn evidence in criminal proceedings).

(8) In this section 'statement' includes any representation of fact, whether made in words or otherwise.

32. Warning to jury

Where on a trial on indictment evidence has been given in accordance with a special measures direction, the judge must give the jury such warning (if any) as the judge considers necessary to ensure that the fact that the direction was given in relation to the witness does not prejudice the accused.

33. Interpretation etc. of Chapter I

(1) In this Chapter—

'eligible witness' means a witness eligible for assistance by virtue of section 16 or 17;

'live link' has the meaning given by section 24(8);

'quality', in relation to the evidence of a witness, shall be construed in accordance with section 16(5);

'special measures direction' means (in accordance with section 19(5)) a direction under section 19.

(2) In this Chapter references to the special measures available in relation to a witness shall be construed in accordance with section 18.

(3) In this Chapter references to a person being able to see or hear, or be seen or heard by, another person are to be read as not applying to the extent that either of them is unable to see or hear by reason of any impairment of eyesight or hearing.

(4) In the case of any proceedings in which there is more than one accused—

(a) any reference to the accused in sections 23 to 28 may be taken by a court, in connection with the giving of a special measures direction, as a reference to all or any of the accused, as the court may determine, and

(b) any such direction may be given on the basis of any such determination.

Chapter II
Protection of Witnesses from Cross-Examination by Accused in Person

General Prohibitions

34. Complainants in proceedings for sexual offences

No person charged with a sexual offence may in any criminal proceedings cross-examine in person a witness who is the complainant, either—

(a) in connection with that offence, or

(b) in connection with any other offence (of whatever nature) with which that person is charged in the proceedings.

35. Child complainants and other child witnesses

(1) No person charged with an offence to which this section applies may in any criminal proceedings cross-examine in person a protected witness, either—

(a) in connection with that offence, or

(b) in connection with any other offence (of whatever nature) with which that person is charged in the proceedings.

(2) For the purposes of subsection (1) a 'protected witness' is a witness who—

    (a) either is the complainant or is alleged to have been a witness to the commission of the offence to which this section applies, and

    (b) either is a child or falls to be cross-examined after giving evidence in chief (whether wholly or in part)—

        (i) by means of a video recording made (for the purposes of section 27) at a time when the witness was a child, or

        (ii) in any other way at any such time.

(3) The offences to which this section applies are—

    (a) any offence under—

        (i) part 1 of the Sexual Offences Act 2003;

        (ii) the Protection of Children Act 1978;

    (b) kidnapping, false imprisonment or an offence under section 1 or 2 of the Child Abduction Act 1984;

    (c) any offence under section 1 of the Children and Young Persons Act 1933;

    (d) any offence (not within any of the preceding paragraphs) which involves an assault on, or injury or a threat of injury to, any person

(4) In this section 'child' means—

    (a) where the offence falls within subsection (3)(a), a person under the age of 17; or

    (b) where the offence falls within subsection (3)(b), (c) or (d), a person under the age of 14.

(5) For the purposes of this section 'witness' includes a witness who is charged with an offence in the proceedings

Prohibition Imposed by the Court

36. Direction prohibiting accused from cross-examining particular witness

(1) This section applies where, in a case where neither of sections 34 and 35 operates to prevent an accused in any criminal proceedings from cross-examining a witness in person—

    (a) the prosecutor makes an application for the court to give a direction under this section in relation to the witness, or

    (b) the court of its own motion raises the issue whether such a direction should be given.

(2) If it appears to the court—

    (a) that the quality of evidence given by the witness on cross-examination—

        (i) is likely to be diminished if the cross-examination (or further cross-examination) is conducted by the accused in person, and

        (ii) would be likely to be improved if a direction were given under this section, and

    (b) that it would not be contrary to the interests of justice to give such a direction,

the court may give a direction prohibiting the accused from cross-examining (or further cross-examining) the witness in person.

(3) In determining whether subsection (2)(a) applies in the case of a witness the court must have regard, in particular, to—

    (a) any views expressed by the witness as to whether or not the witness is content to be cross-examined by the accused in person;

    (b) the nature of the questions likely to be asked, having regard to the issues in the proceedings and the defence case advanced so far (if any);

    (c) any behaviour on the part of the accused at any stage of the proceedings, both generally and in relation to the witness;

    (d) any relationship (of whatever nature) between the witness and the accused;

    (e) whether any person (other than the accused) is or has at any time been charged in the proceedings with a sexual offence or an offence to which section 35 applies, and (if so) whether section 34 or 35 operates or would have operated to prevent that person from cross-examining the witness in person;

    (f) any direction under section 19 which the court has given, or proposes to give, in relation to the witness.

(4) For the purposes of this section—

    (a) 'witness', in relation to an accused, does not include any other person who is charged with an offence in the proceedings; and

    (b) any reference to the quality of a witness's evidence shall be construed in accordance with section 16(5).

37. Further provisions about directions under section 36

(1) Subject to subsection (2), a direction has binding effect from the time it is made until the witness to whom it applies is discharged.

In this section 'direction' means a direction under section 36.

(2) The court may discharge a direction if it appears to the court to be in the interests of justice to do so, and may do so either—

    (a) on an application made by a party to the proceedings, if there has been a material change of circumstances since the relevant time, or

    (b) of its own motion.

(3) In subsection (2) 'the relevant time' means—

    (a) the time when the direction was given, or

    (b) if a previous application has been made under that subsection, the time when the application (or last application) was made.

(4) The court must state in open court its reasons for—

    (a) giving, or

    (b) refusing an application for, or for the discharge of, or

    (c) discharging,

a direction and, if it is a magistrates' court, must cause them to be entered in the register of its proceedings.

(5) Rules of court may make provision—

    (a) for uncontested applications to be determined by the court without a hearing;

    (b) for preventing the renewal of an unsuccessful application for a direction except where there has been a material change of circumstances;

    (c) for expert evidence to be given in connection with an application for, or for discharging, a direction;

(d) for the manner in which confidential or sensitive information is to be treated in connection with such an application and in particular as to its being disclosed to, or withheld from, a party to the proceedings.

Cross-Examination on behalf of Accused

38. Defence representation for purposes of cross-examination

(1) This section applies where an accused is prevented from cross-examining a witness in person by virtue of section 34, 35 or 36

(2) Where it appears to the court that this section applies, it must—
   (a) invite the accused to arrange for a legal representative to act for him for the purpose of cross-examining the witness; and
   (b) require the accused to notify the court, by the end of such period as it may specify, whether a legal representative is to act for him for that purpose.

(3) If by the end of the period mentioned in subsection (2)(b) either—
   (a) the accused has notified the court that no legal representative is to act for him for the purpose of cross-examining the witness, or
   (b) no notification has been received by the court and it appears to the court that no legal representative is to so act,
   the court must consider whether it is necessary in the interests of justice for the witness to be cross-examined by a legal representative appointed to represent the interests of the accused.

(4) If the court decides that it is necessary in the interests of justice for the witness to be so cross-examined, the court must appoint a qualified legal representative (chosen by the court) to cross-examine the witness in the interests of the accused.

(5) A person so appointed shall not be responsible to the accused.

(6) Rules of court may make provision—
   (a) as to the time when, and the manner in which, subsection (2) is to be complied with;
   (b) in connection with the appointment of a legal representative under subsection (4), and in particular for securing that a person so appointed is provided with evidence or other material relating to the proceedings.

(7) Rules of court made in pursuance of subsection (6)(b) may make provision for the application, with such modifications as are specified in the rules, of any of the provisions of—
   (a) Part I of the Criminal Procedure and Investigations Act 1996 (disclosure of material in connection with criminal proceedings), or
   (b) the Sexual Offences (Protected Material) Act 1997.

(8) For the purposes of this section—
   (a) any reference to cross-examination includes (in a case where a direction is given under section 36 after the accused has begun cross-examining the witness) a reference to further cross-examination; and
   (b) 'qualified legal representative' means a legal representative who has a right of audience (within the meaning of the Courts and Legal Services Act 1990) in relation to the proceedings before the court.

39. Warning to jury

(1) Where on a trial on indictment an accused is prevented from cross-examining a witness in person by virtue of section 34, 35 or 36, the judge must give the jury such warning (if any) as the judge considers necessary to ensure that the accused is not prejudiced—

    (a) by any inferences that might be drawn from the fact that the accused has been prevented from cross-examining the witness in person;

    (b) where the witness has been cross-examined by a legal representative appointed under section 38(4), by the fact that the cross-examination was carried out by such a legal representative and not by a person acting as the accused's own legal representative.

(2) Subsection (8)(a) of section 38 applies for the purposes of this section as it applies for the purposes of section 38.

40. Funding of defence representation

(1) In section 19(3) of the Prosecution of Offences Act 1985 (regulations authorising payments out of central funds), after paragraph (d) there shall be inserted—

    '(e) to cover the proper fee or costs of a legal representative appointed under section 38(4) of the Youth Justice and Criminal Evidence Act 1999 (defence representation for purposes of cross-examination) and any expenses properly incurred in providing such a person with evidence or other material in connection with his appointmen.'

(2) In section 21(3) of the Legal Aid Act 1988 (cases where, subject to means, representation must be granted), after paragraph (d) there shall be inserted—

    '(e) where a person is prevented from conducting any cross-examination as mentioned in section 38(1) of the Youth Justice and Criminal Evidence Act 1999 (defence representation for purposes of cross-examination), for conducting the cross-examination on behalf of that person (otherwise than as a person appointed under section 38(4) of that Act).'

CHAPTER III

PROTECTION OF COMPLAINANTS IN PROCEEDINGS FOR SEXUAL OFFENCES

41. Restriction on evidence or questions about complainant's sexual history

(1) If at a trial a person is charged with a sexual offence, then, except with the leave of the court—

    (a) no evidence may be adduced, and

    (b) no question may be asked in cross-examination,

by or on behalf of any accused at the trial, about any sexual behaviour of the complainant.

(2) The court may give leave in relation to any evidence or question only on an application made by or on behalf of an accused, (and may not give such leave unless it is satisfied—

    (a) that subsection (3) or (5) applies, and

    (b) that a refusal of leave might have the result of rendering unsafe a conclusion of the jury or (as the case may be) the court on any relevant issue in the case.

(3) This subsection applies if the evidence or question relates to a relevant issue in the case and either—

    (a) that issue is not an issue of consent; or

    (b) it is an issue of consent and the sexual behaviour of the complainant to which the evidence or question relates is alleged to have taken place at or about the same time as the event which is the subject matter of the charge against the accused; or

    (c) it is an issue of consent and the sexual behaviour of the complainant to which the evidence or question relates is alleged to have been, in any respect, so similar—

        (i) to any sexual behaviour of the complainant which (according to evidence adduced or to be adduced by or on behalf of the accused) took place as part of the event which is the subject matter of the charge against the accused, or

        (ii) to any other sexual behaviour of the complainant which (according to such evidence) took place at or about the same time as that event,

    that the similarity cannot reasonably be explained as a coincidence.

(4) For the purposes of subsection (3) no evidence or question shall be regarded as relating to a relevant issue in the case if it appears to the court to be reasonable to assume that the purpose (or main purpose) for which it would be adduced or asked is to establish or elicit material for impugning the credibility of the complainant as a witness.

(5) This subsection applies if the evidence or question—

    (a) relates to any evidence adduced by the prosecution about any sexual behaviour of the complainant; and

    (b) in the opinion of the court, would go no further than is necessary to enable the evidence adduced by the prosecution to be rebutted or explained by or on behalf of the accused.

(6) For the purposes of subsections (3) and (5) the evidence or question must relate to a specific instance (or specific instances) of alleged sexual behaviour on the part of the complainant (and accordingly nothing in those subsections is capable of applying in relation to the evidence or question to the extent that it does not so relate).

(7) Where this section applies in relation to a trial by virtue of the fact that one or more of a number of persons charged in the proceedings is or are charged with a sexual offence—

    (a) it shall cease to apply in relation to the trial if the prosecutor decides not to proceed with the case against that person or those persons in respect of that charge; but

    (b) it shall not cease to do so in the event of that person or those persons pleading guilty to, or being convicted of, that charge.

(8) Nothing in this section authorises any evidence to be adduced or any question to be asked which cannot be adduced or asked apart from this section.

42. Interpretation and application of section 41

(1) In section 41—

    (a) 'relevant issue in the case' means any issue falling to be proved by the prosecution or defence in the trial of the accused;

(b) 'issue of consent' means any issue whether the complainant in fact consented to the conduct constituting the offence with which the accused is charged (and accordingly does not include any issue as to the belief of the accused that the complainant so consented);

(c) 'sexual behaviour' means any sexual behaviour or other sexual experience, whether or not involving any accused or other person, but excluding (except in section 41(3)(c)(i) and (5)(a)) anything alleged to have taken place as part of the event which is the subject matter of the charge against the accused; and

(d) subject to any order made under subsection (2), 'sexual offence' shall be construed in accordance with section 62.

(2) The Secretary of State may by order make such provision as he considers appropriate for adding or removing, for the purposes of section 41, any offence to or from the offences which are sexual offences for the purposes of this Act by virtue of section 62.

(3) Section 41 applies in relation to the following proceedings as it applies to a trial, namely—

(a) proceedings before a magistrates' court inquiring into an offence as examining justices,

(b) the hearing of an application under paragraph 5(1) of Schedule 6 to the Criminal Justice Act 1991 (application to dismiss charge following notice of transfer of case to Crown Court),

(c) the hearing of an application under paragraph 2(1) of Schedule 3 to the Crime and Disorder Act 1998 (application to dismiss charge by person sent for trial under section 51 of that Act),

(d) any hearing held, between conviction and sentencing, for the purpose of determining matters relevant to the court's decision as to how the accused is to be dealt with, and

(e) the hearing of an appeal,

and references (in section 41 or this section) to a person charged with an offence accordingly include a person convicted of an offence.

43. Procedure on applications under section 41

(1) An application for leave shall be heard in private and in the absence of the complainant.

In this section 'leave' means leave under section 41.

(2) Where such an application has been determined, the court must state in open court (but in the absence of the jury, if there is one)—

(a) its reasons for giving, or refusing, leave, and

(b) if it gives leave, the extent to which evidence may be adduced or questions asked in pursuance of the leave, and, if it is a magistrates' court, must cause those matters to be entered in the register of its proceedings.

(3) Rules of court may make provision—

(a) requiring applications for leave to specify, in relation to each item of evidence or question to which they relate, particulars of the grounds on which it is asserted that leave should be given by virtue of subsection (3) or (5) of section 41;

(b) enabling the court to request a party to the proceedings to provide the court with information which it considers would assist it in determining an application for leave;

(c) for the manner in which confidential or sensitive information is to be treated in connection with such an application, and in particular as to its being disclosed to, or withheld from, parties to the proceedings.

CHAPTER IV

REPORTING RESTRICTIONS

Reporting Restrictions Relating to Persons under 18

44. Restrictions on reporting alleged offences involving persons under 18

(1) This section applies (subject to subsection (3)) where a criminal investigation has begun in respect of—

    (a) an alleged offence against the law of—

        (i) England and Wales, or

        (ii) Northern Ireland; or

    (b) an alleged civil offence (other than an offence falling within paragraph (a)) committed (whether or not in the United Kingdom) by a person subject to service law.

(2) No matter relating to any person involved in the offence shall while he is under the age of 18 be included in any publication if it is likely to lead members of the public to identify him as a person involved in the offence.

(3) The restrictions imposed by subsection (2) cease to apply once there are proceedings in a court (whether a court in England and Wales, a service court or a court in Northern Ireland) in respect of the offence.

(4) For the purposes of subsection (2) any reference to a person involved in the offence is to—

    (a) a person by whom the offence is alleged to have been committed; or

    (b) if this paragraph applies to the publication in question by virtue of subsection (5)—

        (i) a person against or in respect of whom the offence is alleged to have been committed, or

        (ii) a person who is alleged to have been a witness to the commission of the offence;

except that paragraph (b)(i) does not include a person in relation to whom section 1 of the Sexual Offences (Amendment) Act 1992 (anonymity of victims of certain sexual offences) applies in connection with the offence.

(5) Subsection (4)(b) applies to a publication if—

    (a) where it is a relevant programme, it is transmitted, or

    (b) in the case of any other publication, it is published,

on or after such date as may be specified in an order made by the Secretary of State.

(6) The matters relating to a person in relation to which the restrictions imposed by subsection (2) apply (if their inclusion in any publication is likely to have the result mentioned in that subsection) include in particular—

    (a) his name,

    (b) his address,

    (c) the identity of any school or other educational establishment attended by him,

    (d) the identity of any place of work, and

    (e) any still or moving picture of him.

(7) Any appropriate criminal court may by order dispense, to any extent specified in the order, with the restrictions imposed by subsection (2) in relation to a person if it is satisfied that it is necessary in the interests of justice to do so.

(8) However, when deciding whether to make such an order dispensing (to any extent) with the restrictions imposed by subsection (2) in relation to a person, the court shall have regard to the welfare of that person.

(9) In subsection (7) 'appropriate criminal court' means—

    (a) in a case where this section applies by virtue of subsection (1)(a)(i) or (ii), any court in England and Wales or (as the case may be) in Northern Ireland which has any jurisdiction in, or in relation to, any criminal proceedings (but not a service court unless the offence is alleged to have been committed by a person subject to service law);

    (b) in a case where this section applies by virtue of subsection (1)(b), any court falling within paragraph (a) or a service court.

(10) The power under subsection (7) of a magistrates' court in England and Wales may be exercised by a single justice

(11) In the case of a decision of a magistrates' court in England and Wales, or a court of summary jurisdiction in Northern Ireland, to make or refuse to make an order under subsection (7), the following persons, namely—

    (a) any person who was a party to the proceedings on the application for the order, and

    (b) with the leave of the Crown Court, any other person,

may, in accordance with rules of court, appeal to the Crown Court against that decision or appear or be represented at the hearing of such an appeal.

(12) On such an appeal the Crown Court—

    (a) may make such order as is necessary to give effect to its determination of the appeal; and

    (b) may also make such incidental or consequential orders as appear to it to be just.

(13) In this section—

    (a) 'civil offence' means an act or omission which, if committed in England and Wales, would be an offence against the law of England and Wales;

    (b) any reference to a criminal investigation, in relation to an alleged offence, is to an investigation conducted by police officers, or other persons charged with the duty of investigating offences, with a view to it being ascertained whether a person should be charged with the offence;

    (c) any reference to a person subject to service law is to—

        (i) a person subject to military law, air-force law or the Naval Discipline Act 1957, or

        (ii) any other person to whom provisions of Part II of the Army Act 1955, Part II of the Air Force Act 1955 or Parts I and II of the Naval Discipline Act 1957 apply (whether with or without any modifications).

45. Power to restrict reporting of criminal proceedings involving persons under 18

(1) This section applies (subject to subsection (2)) in relation to—
- (a) any criminal proceedings in any court (other than a service court) in England and Wales or Northern Ireland; and
- (b) any proceedings (whether in the United Kingdom or elsewhere) in any service court.

(2) This section does not apply in relation to any proceedings to which section 49 of the Children and Young Persons Act 1933 applies.

(3) The court may direct that no matter relating to any person concerned in the proceedings shall while he is under the age of 18 be included in any publication if it is likely to lead members of the public to identify him as a person concerned in the proceedings.

(4) The court or an appellate court may by direction ('an excepting direction') dispense, to any extent specified in the excepting direction, with the restrictions imposed by a direction under subsection (3) if it is satisfied that it is necessary in the interests of justice to do so.

(5) The court or an appellate court may also by direction ('an excepting direction') dispense, to any extent specified in the excepting direction, with the restrictions imposed by a direction under subsection (3) if it is satisfied—
- (a) that their effect is to impose a substantial and unreasonable restriction on the reporting of the proceedings, and
- (b) that it is in the public interest to remove or relax that restriction;

but no excepting direction shall be given under this subsection by reason only of the fact that the proceedings have been determined in any way or have been abandoned.

(6) When deciding whether to make—
- (a) a direction under subsection (3) in relation to a person, or
- (b) an excepting direction under subsection (4) or (5) by virtue of which the restrictions imposed by a direction under subsection (3) would be dispensed with (to any extent) in relation to a person,

the court or (as the case may be) the appellate court shall have regard to the welfare of that person.

(7) For the purposes of subsection (3) any reference to a person concerned in the proceedings is to a person—
- (a) against or in respect of whom the proceedings are taken, or
- (b) who is a witness in the proceedings.

(8) The matters relating to a person in relation to which the restrictions imposed by a direction under subsection (3) apply (if their inclusion in any publication is likely to have the result mentioned in that subsection) include in particular—
- (a) his name,
- (b) his address,
- (c) the identity of any school or other educational establishment attended by him,
- (d) the identity of any place of work, and
- (e) any still or moving picture of him.

(9) A direction under subsection (3) may be revoked by the court or an appellate court

(10) An excepting direction—

    (a) may be given at the time the direction under subsection (3) is given or subsequently; and

    (b) may be varied or revoked by the court or an appellate court.

(11) In this section 'appellate court', in relation to any proceedings in a court, means a court dealing with an appeal (including an appeal by way of case stated) arising out of the proceedings or with any further appeal.

Reports Relating to Adult Witnesses

46. Power to restrict reports about certain adult witnesses in criminal proceedings

(1) This section applies where—

    (a) in any criminal proceedings in any court (other than a service court) in England and Wales or Northern Ireland, or

    (b) in any proceedings (whether in the United Kingdom or elsewhere) in any service court,

a party to the proceedings makes an application for the court to give a reporting direction in relation to a witness in the proceedings (other than the accused) who has attained the age of 18.

In this section 'reporting direction' has the meaning given by subsection (6).

(2) If the court determines—

    (a) that the witness is eligible for protection, and

    (b) that giving a reporting direction in relation to the witness is likely to improve—

        (i) the quality of evidence given by the witness, or

        (ii) the level of co-operation given by the witness to any party to the proceedings in connection with that party's preparation of its case,

the court may give a reporting direction in relation to the witness.

(3) For the purposes of this section a witness is eligible for protection if the court is satisfied—

    (a) that the quality of evidence given by the witness, or

    (b) the level of co-operation given by the witness to any party to the proceedings in connection with that party's preparation of its case,

is likely to be diminished by reason of fear or distress on the part of the witness in connection with being identified by members of the public as a witness in the proceedings.

(4) In determining whether a witness is eligible for protection the court must take into account, in particular—

    (a) the nature and alleged circumstances of the offence to which the proceedings relate;

    (b) the age of the witness;

    (c) such of the following matters as appear to the court to be relevant, namely—

        (i) the social and cultural background and ethnic origins of the witness,

        (ii) the domestic and employment circumstances of the witness, and

        (iii) any religious beliefs or political opinions of the witness;

    (d) any behaviour towards the witness on the part of—
       (i) the accused,
      (ii) members of the family or associates of the accused, or
     (iii) any other person who is likely to be an accused or a witness in the proceedings.

(5) In determining that question the court must in addition consider any views expressed by the witness.

(6) For the purposes of this section a reporting direction in relation to a witness is a direction that no matter relating to the witness shall during the witness's lifetime be included in any publication if it is likely to lead members of the public to identify him as being a witness in the proceedings.

(7) The matters relating to a witness in relation to which the restrictions imposed by a reporting direction apply (if their inclusion in any publication is likely to have the result mentioned in subsection (6)) include in particular—
    (a) the witness's name,
    (b) the witness's address,
    (c) the identity of any educational establishment attended by the witness,
    (d) the identity of any place of work, and
    (e) any still or moving picture of the witness.

(8) In determining whether to give a reporting direction the court shall consider—
    (a) whether it would be in the interests of justice to do so, and
    (b) the public interest in avoiding the imposition of a substantial and unreasonable restriction on the reporting of the proceedings.

(9) The court or an appellate court may by direction ('an excepting direction') dispense, to any extent specified in the excepting direction, with the restrictions imposed by a reporting direction if—
    (a) it is satisfied that it is necessary in the interests of justice to do so, or
    (b) it is satisfied—
       (i) that the effect of those restrictions is to impose a substantial and unreasonable restriction on the reporting of the proceedings, and
      (ii) that it is in the public interest to remove or relax that restriction;
    but no excepting direction shall be given under paragraph (b) by reason only of the fact that the proceedings have been determined in any way or have been abandoned.

(10) A reporting direction may be revoked by the court or an appellate court.

(11) An excepting direction—
    (a) may be given at the time the reporting direction is given or subsequently; and
    (b) may be varied or revoked by the court or an appellate court.

(12) In this section—
    (a) 'appellate court', in relation to any proceedings in a court, means a court dealing with an appeal (including an appeal by way of case stated) arising out of the proceedings or with any further appeal;
    (b) references to the quality of a witness's evidence are to its quality in terms of completeness, coherence and accuracy (and for this purpose 'coherence' refers to a witness's ability in giving evidence to give answers which address

the questions put to the witness and can be understood both individually and collectively);

(c) references to the preparation of the case of a party to any proceedings include, where the party is the prosecution, the carrying out of investigations into any offence at any time charged in the proceedings.

Reports Relating to Directions under Chapter I or II

47. Restrictions on reporting directions under Chapter I or II

(1) Except as provided by this section, no publication shall include a report of a matter falling within subsection (2).

(2) The matters falling within this subsection are—

(a) a direction under section 19 or 36 or an order discharging, or (in the case of a direction under section 19) varying, such a direction;

(b) proceedings—

(i) on an application for such a direction or order, or

(ii) where the court acts of its own motion to determine whether to give or make any such direction or order.

(3) The court dealing with a matter falling within subsection (2) may order that subsection (1) is not to apply, or is not to apply to a specified extent, to a report of that matter.

(4) Where—

(a) there is only one accused in the relevant proceedings, and

(b) he objects to the making of an order under subsection (3),

the court shall make the order if (and only if) satisfied after hearing the representations of the accused that it is in the interests of justice to do so; and if the order is made it shall not apply to the extent that a report deals with any such objections or representations.

(5) Where—

(a) there are two or more accused in the relevant proceedings, and

(b) one or more of them object to the making of an order under subsection (3),

the court shall make the order if (and only if) satisfied after hearing the representations of each of the accused that it is in the interests of justice to do so; and if the order is made it shall not apply to the extent that a report deals with any such objections or representations.

(6) Subsection (1) does not apply to the inclusion in a publication of a report of matters after the relevant proceedings are either—

(a) determined (by acquittal, conviction or otherwise), or

(b) abandoned,

in relation to the accused or (if there is more than one) in relation to each of the accused.

(7) In this section 'the relevant proceedings' means the proceedings to which any such direction as is mentioned in subsection (2) relates or would relate.

(8) Nothing in this section affects any prohibition or restriction by virtue of any other enactment on the inclusion of matter in a publication.

Other Restrictions

48. Amendments relating to other reporting restrictions

Schedule 2, which contains amendments relating to reporting restrictions under—

(a) the Children and Young Persons Act 1933,

(b) the Sexual Offences (Amendment) Act 1976,

(c) the Sexual Offences (Northern Ireland) Order 1978,

(d) the Sexual Offences (Amendment) Act 1992, and

(e) the Criminal Justice (Northern Ireland) Order 1994,

shall have effect.

Offences

49. Offences under Chapter IV

(1) This section applies if a publication—

    (a) includes any matter in contravention of section 44(2) or of a direction under section 45(3) or 46(2); or

    (b) includes a report in contravention of section 47

(2) Where the publication is a newspaper or periodical, any proprietor, any editor and any publisher of the newspaper or periodical is guilty of an offence.

(3) Where the publication is a relevant programme—

    (a) any body corporate or Scottish partnership engaged in providing the programme service in which the programme is included, and

    (b) any person having functions in relation to the programme corresponding to those of an editor of a newspaper,

is guilty of an offence.

(4) In the case of any other publication, any person publishing it is guilty of an offence.

(5) A person guilty of an offence under this section is liable on summary conviction to a fine not exceeding level 5 on the standard scale.

(6) Proceedings for an offence under this section in respect of a publication falling within subsection (1)(b) may not be instituted—

    (a) in England and Wales otherwise than by or with the consent of the Attorney General, or

    (b) in Northern Ireland otherwise than by or with the consent of the Attorney General for Northern Ireland.

50. Defences

(1) Where a person is charged with an offence under section 49 it shall be a defence to prove that at the time of the alleged offence he was not aware, and neither suspected nor had reason to suspect, that the publication included the matter or report in question.

(2) Where—

    (a) a person is charged with an offence under section 49, and

    (b) the offence relates to the inclusion of any matter in a publication in contravention of section 44(2), it shall be a defence to prove that at the time of the alleged offence he was not aware, and neither suspected nor had reason to suspect, that the criminal investigation in question had begun.

(3) Where—

    (a) paragraphs (a) and (b) of subsection (2) apply, and

    (b) the contravention of section 44(2) does not relate to either—

        (i) the person by whom the offence mentioned in that provision is alleged to have been committed, or

        (ii) (where that offence is one in relation to which section 1 of the Sexual Offences (Amendment) Act 1992 applies) a person who is alleged to be a witness to the commission of the offence,

it shall be a defence to show to the satisfaction of the court that the inclusion in the publication of the matter in question was in the public interest on the ground that, to the extent that they operated to prevent that matter from being so included, the effect of the restrictions imposed by section 44(2) was to impose a substantial and unreasonable restriction on the reporting of matters connected with that offence.

(4) Subsection (5) applies where—

    (a) paragraphs (a) and (b) of subsection (2) apply, and

    (b) the contravention of section 44(2) relates to a person ('the protected person') who is neither—

        (i) the person mentioned in subsection (3)(b)(i), nor

        (ii) a person within subsection (3)(b)(ii) who is under the age of 16.

(5) In such a case it shall be a defence, subject to subsection (6), to prove that written consent to the inclusion of the matter in question in the publication had been given—

    (a) by an appropriate person, if at the time when the consent was given the protected person was under the age of 16, or

    (b) by the protected person, if that person was aged 16 or 17 at that time,

and (where the consent was given by an appropriate person) that written notice had been previously given to that person drawing to his attention the need to consider the welfare of the protected person when deciding whether to give consent.

(6) The defence provided by subsection (5) is not available if—

    (a) (where the consent was given by an appropriate person) it is proved that written or other notice withdrawing the consent—

        (i) was given to the appropriate recipient by any other appropriate person or by the protected person, and

        (ii) was so given in sufficient time to enable the inclusion in the publication of the matter in question to be prevented; or

    (b) subsection (8) applies

(7) Where—

    (a) a person is charged with an offence under section 49, and

    (b) the offence relates to the inclusion of any matter in a publication in contravention of a direction under section 46(2), it shall be a defence, unless subsection (8) applies, to prove that the person in relation to whom the direction was given had given written consent to the inclusion of that matter in the publication.

(8) Written consent is not a defence if it is proved that any person interfered—

    (a) with the peace or comfort of the person giving the consent, or

    (b) (where the consent was given by an appropriate person) with the peace or comfort of either that person or the protected person,

with intent to obtain the consent.

(9) In this section—

'an appropriate person' means (subject to subsections (10) to (12))—

    (a) in England and Wales or Northern Ireland, a person who is a parent or guardian of the protected person,

    (b) in Scotland, a person who has parental responsibilities (within the meaning of section 1(3) of the Children (Scotland) Act 1995) in relation to the protected person;

'guardian', in relation to the protected person, means any person who is not a parent of the protected person but who has parental responsibility for the protected person within the meaning of—

    (a) (in England and Wales) the Children Act 1989, or

    (b) (in Northern Ireland) the Children (Northern Ireland) Order 1995.

(10) Where the protected person is (within the meaning of the Children Act 1989) a child who is looked after by a local authority, 'an appropriate person' means a person who is—

    (a) a representative of that authority, or

    (b) a parent or guardian of the protected person with whom the protected person is allowed to live.

(11) Where the protected person is (within the meaning of the Children (Northern Ireland) Order 1995) a child who is looked after by an authority, 'an appropriate person' means a person who is—

    (a) an officer of that authority, or

    (b) a parent or guardian of the protected person with whom the protected person is allowed to live.

(12) Where the protected person is (within the meaning of section 17(6) of the Children (Scotland) Act 1995) a child who is looked after by a local authority, 'an appropriate person' means a person who is—

    (a) a representative of that authority, or

    (b) a person who has parental responsibilities (within the meaning of section 1(3) of that Act) in relation to the protected person and with whom the protected person is allowed to live.

(13) However, no person by whom the offence mentioned in section 44(2) is alleged to have been committed is, by virtue of subsections (9) to (12), an appropriate person for the purposes of this section.

(14) In this section 'the appropriate recipient', in relation to a notice under subsection (6)(a), means—

    (a) the person to whom the notice giving consent was given,

    (b) (if different) the person by whom the matter in question was published, or

    (c) any other person exercising, on behalf of the person mentioned in paragraph
        (b), any responsibility in relation to the publication of that matter;
and for this purpose 'person' includes a body of persons and a partnership.

51. Offences committed by bodies corporate or Scottish partnerships

(1) If an offence under section 49 committed by a body corporate is proved—
    (a) to have been committed with the consent or connivance of, or
    (b) to be attributable to any neglect on the part of,an officer, the officer as well as
        the body corporate is guilty of the offence and liable to be proceeded against
        and punished accordingly.

(2) In subsection (1) 'officer' means a director, manager, secretary or other similar
officer of the body, or a person purporting to act in any such capacity.

(3) If the affairs of a body corporate are managed by its members, 'director' in subsection (2) means a member of that body.

(4) Where an offence under section 49 is committed by a Scottish partnership and
is proved to have been committed with the consent or connivance of a partner,
he as well as the partnership shall be guilty of the offence and shall be liable to
be proceeded against and punished accordingly.

Supplementary

52. Decisions as to public interest for purposes of Chapter IV

(1) Where for the purposes of any provision of this Chapter it falls to a court to
determine whether anything is (or, as the case may be, was) in the public interest, the court must have regard, in particular, to the matters referred to in subsection (2) (so far as relevant).

(2) Those matters are—
    (a) the interest in each of the following—
        (i) the open reporting of crime,
        (ii) the open reporting of matters relating to human health or safety, and
        (iii) the prevention and exposure of miscarriages of justice;
    (b) the welfare of any person in relation to whom the relevant restrictions
        imposed by or under this Chapter apply or would apply (or, as the case may
        be, applied); and
    (c) any views expressed—
        (i) by an appropriate person on behalf of a person within paragraph (b)
        who is under the age of 16 ('the protected person'), or
        (ii) by a person within that paragraph who has attained that age

(3) In subsection (2) 'an appropriate person', in relation to the protected person, has
the same meaning as it has for the purposes of section 50.

CHAPTER V
COMPETENCE OF WITNESSES AND CAPACITY TO BE SWORN
Competence of Witnesses

53. Competence of witnesses to give evidence

(1) At every stage in criminal proceedings all persons are (whatever their age) competent to give evidence.

(2) Subsection (1) has effect subject to subsections (3) and (4).

(3) A person is not competent to give evidence in criminal proceedings if it appears to the court that he is not a person who is able to—

   (a) understand questions put to him as a witness, and

   (b) give answers to them which can be understood.

(4) A person charged in criminal proceedings is not competent to give evidence in the proceedings for the prosecution (whether he is the only person, or is one of two or more persons, charged in the proceedings).

(5) In subsection (4) the reference to a person charged in criminal proceedings does not include a person who is not, or is no longer, liable to be convicted of any offence in the proceedings (whether as a result of pleading guilty or for any other reason).

54. Determining competence of witnesses

(1) Any question whether a witness in criminal proceedings is competent to give evidence in the proceedings, whether raised—

   (a) by a party to the proceedings, or

   (b) by the court of its own motion,

shall be determined by the court in accordance with this section.

(2) It is for the party calling the witness to satisfy the court that, on a balance of probabilities, the witness is competent to give evidence in the proceedings.

(3) In determining the question mentioned in subsection (1) the court shall treat the witness as having the benefit of any directions under section 19 which the court has given, or proposes to give, in relation to the witness.

(4) Any proceedings held for the determination of the question shall take place in the absence of the jury (if there is one).

(5) Expert evidence may be received on the question.

(6) Any questioning of the witness (where the court considers that necessary) shall be conducted by the court in the presence of the parties.

Giving of Sworn or Unsworn Evidence

55. Determining whether witness to be sworn

(1) Any question whether a witness in criminal proceedings may be sworn for the purpose of giving evidence on oath, whether raised:

   (a) by a party to the proceedings, or

   (b) by the court of its own motion,

shall be determined by the court in accordance with this section.

(2) The witness may not be sworn for that purpose unless—

   (a) he has attained the age of 14, and

   (b) he has a sufficient appreciation of the solemnity of the occasion and of the particular responsibility to tell the truth which is involved in taking an oath.

(3) The witness shall, if he is able to give intelligible testimony, be presumed to have a sufficient appreciation of those matters if no evidence tending to show the contrary is adduced (by any party).

(4) If any such evidence is adduced, it is for the party seeking to have the witness sworn to satisfy the court that, on a balance of probabilities, the witness has

attained the age of 14 and has a sufficient appreciation of the matters mentioned in subsection (2)(b).

(5) Any proceedings held for the determination of the question mentioned in subsection (1) shall take place in the absence of the jury (if there is one).

(6) Expert evidence may be received on the question.

(7) Any questioning of the witness (where the court considers that necessary) shall be conducted by the court in the presence of the parties.

(8) For the purposes of this section a person is able to give intelligible testimony if he is able to—

(a) understand questions put to him as a witness, and

(b) give answers to them which can be understood.

56. Reception of unsworn evidence

(1) Subsections (2) and (3) apply to a person (of any age) who—

(a) is competent to give evidence in criminal proceedings, but

(b) (by virtue of section 55(2)) is not permitted to be sworn for the purpose of giving evidence on oath in such proceedings.

(2) The evidence in criminal proceedings of a person to whom this subsection applies shall be given unsworn.

(3) A deposition of unsworn evidence given by a person to whom this subsection applies may be taken for the purposes of criminal proceedings as if that evidence had been given on oath.

(4) A court in criminal proceedings shall accordingly receive in evidence any evidence given unsworn in pursuance of subsection (2) or (3).

(5) Where a person ('the witness') who is competent to give evidence in criminal proceedings gives evidence in such proceedings unsworn, no conviction, verdict or finding in those proceedings shall be taken to be unsafe for the purposes of any of sections 2(1), 13(1) and 16(1) of the Criminal Appeal Act 1968 (grounds for allowing appeals) by reason only that it appears to the Court of Appeal that the witness was a person falling within section 55(2) (and should accordingly have given his evidence on oath).

57. Penalty for giving false unsworn evidence

(1) This section applies where a person gives unsworn evidence in criminal proceedings in pursuance of section 56(2) or (3).

(2) If such a person wilfully gives false evidence in such circumstances that, had the evidence been given on oath, he would have been guilty of perjury, he shall be guilty of an offence and liable on summary conviction to—

(a) imprisonment for a term not exceeding 6 months, or

(b) a fine not exceeding £1,000,

or both.

(3) In relation to a person under the age of 14, subsection (2) shall have effect as if for the words following 'on summary conviction' there were substituted 'to a fine not exceeding £250'.

Appendix B
Mental Capacity Act 2005
Part I, Sections 1 to 8

1. The principles

(1) The following principles apply for the purposes of this Act.

(2) A person must be assumed to have capacity unless it is established that he lacks capacity.

(3) A person is not to be treated as unable to make a decision unless all practicable steps to help him to do so have been taken without success.

(4) A person is not to be treated as unable to make a decision merely because he makes an unwise decision.

(5) An act done, or decision made, under this Act for or on behalf of a person who lacks capacity must be done, or made, in his best interests.

(6) Before the act is done, or the decision is made, regard must be had to whether the purpose for which it is needed can be as effectively achieved in a way that is less restrictive of the person's rights and freedom of action.

2. People who lack capacity

(1) For the purposes of this Act, a person lacks capacity in relation to a matter if at the material time he is unable to make a decision for himself in relation to the matter because of an impairment of, or a disturbance in the functioning of, the mind or brain.

(2) It does not matter whether the impairment or disturbance is permanent or temporary.

(3) A lack of capacity cannot be established merely by reference to—
   (a) a person's age or appearance, or
   (b) a condition of his, or an aspect of his behaviour, which might lead others to make unjustified assumptions about his capacity.

(4) In proceedings under this Act or any other enactment, any question whether a person lacks capacity within the meaning of this Act must be decided on the balance of probabilities.

(5) No power which a person ('D') may exercise under this Act—
   (a) in relation to a person who lacks capacity, or
   (b) where D reasonably thinks that a person lacks capacity,
   is exercisable in relation to a person under 16.

(6) Subsection (5) is subject to section 18(3).

3. Inability to make decisions

(1) For the purposes of section 2, a person is unable to make a decision for himself if he is unable—

    (a) to understand the information relevant to the decision,

    (b) to retain that information,

    (c) to use or weigh that information as part of the process of making the decision, or

    (d) to communicate his decision (whether by talking, using sign language or any other means).

(2) A person is not to be regarded as unable to understand the information relevant to a decision if he is able to understand an explanation of it given to him in a way that is appropriate to his circumstances (using simple language, visual aids or any other means).

(3) The fact that a person is able to retain the information relevant to a decision for a short period only does not prevent him from being regarded as able to make the decision.

(4) The information relevant to a decision includes information about the reasonably foreseeable consequences of—

    (a) deciding one way or another, or

    (b) failing to make the decision.

4. Best interests

(1) In determining for the purposes of this Act what is in a person's best interests, the person making the determination must not make it merely on the basis of—

    (a) the person's age or appearance, or

    (b) a condition of his, or an aspect of his behaviour, which might lead others to make unjustified assumptions about what might be in his best interests.

(2) The person making the determination must consider all the relevant circumstances and, in particular, take the following steps.

(3) He must consider—

    (a) whether it is likely that the person will at some time have capacity in relation to the matter in question, and

    (b) if it appears likely that he will, when that is likely to be.

(4) He must, so far as reasonably practicable, permit and encourage the person to participate, or to improve his ability to participate, as fully as possible in any act done for him and any decision affecting him

(5) Where the determination relates to life-sustaining treatment he must not, in considering whether the treatment is in the best interests of the person concerned, be motivated by a desire to bring about his death.

(6) He must consider, so far as is reasonably ascertainable—

    (a) the person's past and present wishes and feelings (and, in particular, any relevant written statement made by him when he had capacity),

    (b) the beliefs and values that would be likely to influence his decision if he had capacity, and

    (c) the other factors that he would be likely to consider if he were able to do so.

(7) He must take into account, if it is practicable and appropriate to consult them, the views of—

    (a) anyone named by the person as someone to be consulted on the matter in question or on matters of that kind,

    (b) anyone engaged in caring for the person or interested in his welfare,

    (c) any donee of a lasting power of attorney granted by the person, and

    (d) any deputy appointed for the person by the court,
as to what would be in the person's best interests and, in particular, as to the matters mentioned in subsection (6).

(8) The duties imposed by subsections (1) to (7) also apply in relation to the exercise of any powers which—

    (a) are exercisable under a lasting power of attorney, or

    (b) are exercisable by a person under this Act where he reasonably believes that another person lacks capacity.

(9) In the case of an act done, or a decision made, by a person other than the court, there is sufficient compliance with this section if (having complied with the requirements of subsections (1) to (7)) he reasonably believes that what he does or decides is in the best interests of the person concerned.

(10) 'Life-sustaining treatment' means treatment which in the view of a person providing health care for the person concerned is necessary to sustain life.

(11) 'Relevant circumstances' are those—

    (a) of which the person making the determination is aware, and

    (b) which it would be reasonable to regard as relevant.

5. Acts in connection with care or treatment

(1) If a person ('D') does an act in connection with the care or treatment of another person ('P'), the act is one to which this section applies if—

    (a) before doing the act, D takes reasonable steps to establish whether P lacks capacity in relation to the matter in question, and

    (b) when doing the act, D reasonably believes—

        (i)   that P lacks capacity in relation to the matter, and

        (ii) that it will be in P's best interests for the act to be done.

(2) D does not incur any liability in relation to the act that he would not have incurred if P—

    (a) had had capacity to consent in relation to the matter, and

    (b) had consented to D's doing the act.

(3) Nothing in this section excludes a person's civil liability for loss or damage, or his criminal liability, resulting from his negligence in doing the act.

(4) Nothing in this section affects the operation of sections 24 to 26 (advance decisions to refuse treatment).

6. Limitations on Section 5 acts

(1) If D does an act that is intended to restrain P, it is not an act to which section 5 applies unless two further conditions are satisfied.

(2) The first condition is that D reasonably believes that it is necessary to do the act in order to prevent harm to P.

(3) The second is that the act is a proportionate response to—

    (a) the likelihood of P's suffering harm, and

    (b) the seriousness of that harm.

(4) For the purposes of this section D restrains P if he—

    (a) uses, or threatens to use, force to secure the doing of an act which P resists, or

    (b) restricts P's liberty of movement, whether or not P resists.

(5) But D does more than merely restrain P if he deprives P of his liberty within the meaning of Article 5(1) of the Human Rights Convention (whether or not D is a public authority).

(6) Section 5 does not authorise a person to do an act which conflicts with a decision made, within the scope of his authority and in accordance with this Part, by—

    (a) a donee of a lasting power of attorney granted by P, or

    (b) a deputy appointed for P by the court.

(7) But nothing in subsection (6) stops a person—

    (a) providing life-sustaining treatment, or

    (b) doing any act which he reasonably believes to be necessary to prevent a serious deterioration in P's condition,

while a decision as respects any relevant issue is sought from the court.

7. Payment for necessary goods and services

(1) If necessary goods or services are supplied to a person who lacks capacity to contract for the supply, he must pay a reasonable price for them.

(2) 'Necessary' means suitable to a person's condition in life and to his actual requirements at the time when the goods or services are supplied.

8. Expenditure

(1) If an act to which section 5 applies involves expenditure, it is lawful for D—

    (a) to pledge P's credit for the purpose of the expenditure, and

    (b) to apply money in P's possession for meeting the expenditure.

(2) If the expenditure is borne for P by D, it is lawful for D—

    (a) to reimburse himself out of money in P's possession, or

    (b) to be otherwise indemnified by P.

(3) Subsections (1) and (2) do not affect any power under which (apart from those subsections) a person—

    (a) has lawful control of P's money or other property, and

    (b) has power to spend money for P's benefit.

References

Burton M., Evans R., and Sanders A. (2006), 'Are Special Measures for Vulnerable and Intimidated Witnesses Working?' Evidence from the Criminal Justice Agencies, On-Line Report 01/06 (London, Home Office).

Department for Constitutional Affairs (2007), *Mental Capacity Act 2005 Code of Practice* (London, Department for Constitutional Affairs).

Department for Education and Skills (2006), *Working Together to Safeguard Children: A Guide to Inter-Agency Working to Safeguard and Promote the Welfare of Children* (London, TSO).

Department of Health (2000), *No Secrets: Guidance on Developing and Implementing Multi-Agency Policies and Procedures to Protect Vulnerable Adults from Abuse* (London, Department of Health and Home Office).

Hamlyn B., Phelps A., and Sattar G. (2004), *Key Findings from the Surveys of Vulnerable and Intimidated Witnesses 2000/01 and 2003* (London, Home Office).

Home Office (1989), *Report of the Advisory Group on Video Evidence* (London, Home Office).

—— (1998), *Speaking Up for Justice*. Report of the Interdepartmental Working Group on the Treatment of Vulnerable or Intimidated Witnesses in the Criminal Justice System (London, Home Office).

—— (2001), *Early Special Measures Meetings Between the Police and the Crown Prosecution Service and Meetings Between the Crown Prosecution Service and Vulnerable or Intimidated Witnesses: Practice Guidance* (London, Home Office).

—— (2001), *Provision of Therapy to Child Witnesses Prior to a Criminal Trial: Practice Guidance* (London, Home Office).

—— (2001), *Provision of Therapy to Vulnerable or Intimidated Adult Witnesses Prior to a Criminal Trial: Practice Guidance* (London, Home Office).

—— (2002), *Achieving Best Evidence in Criminal Proceedings: Guidance for Vulnerable or Intimidated Witnesses, Including Children* (London, Home Office).

—— (2002), *Justice for All* (London, Home Office).

—— (2002), *Vulnerable Witnesses: A Police Service Guide* (London, Home Office).

—— (2003), *A New Deal for Victims and Witnesses: National Strategy to Deliver Improved Services* (London, Home Office).

—— (2003), *No Witness, No Justice: Towards a National Strategy for Witnesses*, Report of the Interagency Working Group on Witnesses (London, Home Office).

—— (2007), *Achieving Best Evidence in Criminal Proceedings: Guidance on Interviewing Victims and Witnesses, and using Special Measures* (London, Home Office).

Maynard W. (1994), *Witness Intimidation: Strategies for Prevention*, Police Research Group Crime Prevention and Detection Series Paper 55 (London, Home Office).

National Assembly for Wales (2000), *In Safe Hands: Implementing Adult Protection Procedures in Wales* (Cardiff, National Assembly for Wales).

Office for Criminal Justice Reform (2005), *The Code of Practice for Victims of Crime* (London, Office for Criminal Justice Reform).

—— (2005), *Witness Charter* (Consultation Draft) (London, Office for Criminal Justice Reform).

Westcott H. (1991), 'The Abuse of Disabled Children: A Review of the Literature' 17 *Child Care Health and Development* 243–58.

Index